THE LIFE-CYCLE OF SYNAGOGUE MEMBERSHIP:

A Guide to Recruitment, Integration & Retention

Prepared by
The Task Force on the Unaffiliated
of the
Union of American Hebrew Congregations

ACKNOWLEDGEMENTS

UAHC Task Force on the Unaffiliated
Melvin Merians, Chairman
Rabbi Steven E. Foster, Co-Chairman
Dru Greenwood, Director, UAHC-CCAR Commision
on Reform Jewish Outreach and
Executive Editor
Rabbi Renni S. Altman, Director of Programs
and Editor
Audrey Wilson, Chair of Retention Committee,
Associate Director, UAHC Northeast Council
and Co-Editor

Administrative Staff: Mickey Finn
Cover Design: Bill Cwiekalo

* * *

We express special gratitude to the following members of the Task Force who contributed to the preparation of this resource:

Vicky Farhi
Shirlee Goldman-Herzog
Lois Gutman
Judith Hertz
Myra Ostroff
Dr. Richard Plumb
Dr. Richard Shugarman
Leonard Spring
Irv Wengrow
Mark Werfel

We would like to express our appreciation to the Alban Institute, Inc. and to Church Management, Inc. for allowing us to adapt their materials for our work in synagogues and to the Ida and Howard Wilkoff Department on Synagogue Management of the UAHC for their resources.

We would like to thank those congregations who participated in testing these exercises and those who shared their programs and ideas with us. We would also like to thank all those whose insights and comments were invaluable to our work.

UAHC TASK FORCE ON THE UNAFFILIATED

Rabbi James Bennett
Harold Bobroff
Rabbi Alan Bregman
Bernice Brussel
Dr. Norman Cohen
Fred Curry
Vicky Farhi
Morton Finkelstein
Rabbi Ronne Friedman
Rabbi Stuart M. Geller
Rabbi Gary Glickstein
Rabbi Irwin Goldenberg
Shirlee Goldman-Herzog
Lois Gutman
Robert Hamburger
Judith Hertz
Martin Hertz
Arthur Heyman
Frances Hyman
Rabbi Howard Jaffe
Barry Kugel
Rabbi Steven Leder
Rabbi Harold Loss
May Mass
Rabbi Dennis Math
Rabbi Michael Mayersohn
Rabbi Bernard Mehlman
Alfred Miller
Rabbi John Moscowitz
John Naylor
Myra Ostroff
Dr. Richard Plumb
Gerry Prosnitz
Ruth Reidbord
Rabbi Alvin Reines
Arlene Rephan

Rabbi Donald Rossoff
Lawrence Rothenberg
Dr. Judith Sherman-Asher
Dr. Richard Shugarman
Lawrence Simon
Beverly Singer
Helene Spring
Leonard Spring
John Stern
Norton Stern
Sherrie Stern
J. Jacques Stone
Rabbi Frank Sundheim
Iris Franco Vanek
Pam Waechter
Rabbi Roy Walter
Irv Wengrow
Mark Werfel
Audrey Wilson
Pamella Winter
Norman Yanofsky
Robert Zinman
Rabbi Bernard Zlotowitz
Rabbi Gary Zola

Ex-Officio Members

Joseph Bernstein
Rabbi Howard Bogot
Rabbi Joseph Glaser
Rabbi Alexander Schindler
Rabbi Sanford Seltzer
Rabbi Daniel Syme

CONTENTS

INTRODUCTION

The great rabbi Hillel taught: "Do not separate yourself from the community" (*Pirke Avot* 2:5). Yet, today the vast majority of Jews in North America, some 70% of the Jewish population, according to Dr. Gary Tobin, Director of the Cohen Center for Modern Jewish Studies at Brandeis University, disregards Hillel's teaching and remains apart from the Jewish community by not affiliating with a synagogue. These statistics do not bode well for the future of Judaism in North America. Time and again, studies have shown that Jews who affiliate with synagogues are more involved in Jewish life, both in the community and in their homes, more actively support the State of Israel, are more philanthropic in general and volunteer more of their time than do those who remain unaffiliated. Our future as a Jewish community depends on the participation of Jews in synagogue life; the future of our synagogues depends on their participation as well. The vast numbers of unaffiliated Jews constitute an untapped reservoir of energy and creativity for Reform Judaism.

In 1989, in a visionary act to reverse the foreboding trends in affiliation, Rabbi Alexander Schindler called for the formation of a UAHC Task Force on the Unaffiliated, whose goal would be to actively reach out to the 3 million Jews who currently stand on the periphery of Jewish life and draw them in to the synagogue. The mission of the Task Force is two-fold:

> To reach out to unaffiliated, marginally affiliated and previously affiliated Jews and inspire them to seek a place for themselves within our synagogue community;

> To promote such change in the institutions and temples of Reform Judaism as will render our congregational programs more repsonsive and sensitive to the expressed needs of the unaffiliated.

The first major project of the Task Force has been the creation of the UAHC Privilege Card, a program designed to reach out to the unaffiliated population of young adult Jews, age 22-30. Participating congregations are welcoming young adults into their synagogues by granting them time-limited free memberships or membership at significantly reduced rates. At the same time, these congregations are developing special programs for and responding to the needs of Jews in this age group.

While only approximately one-third of the Jewish population of North America is currently affiliated, 85-90% of Jews *do* affiliate at some point in their adult lives — for the vast majority of Jews, synagogue affiliation is a revolving door phenomenon. And, of the three major Jewish movements in North America, the Reform movement has the shortest lifespan of temple membership. These telling statistics have provided us with a new profile of the unaffiliated Jew: an individual who does affiliate with a synagogue for some time, but who drops that affiliation when it is no longer meaningful. Reaching *out* to the unaffiliated must begin, therefore, by reaching *into* our congregations and creating an environment in which our members want to belong and maintain their membership. We need to ask ourselves why we are losing 55% of the Jewish population who, at least for some time, were connected to the synagogue. What can we do to maintain the commitment of our members and not lose them after their children have completed their religious education?

In seeking answers to these questions, we have learned that membership retention cannot be considered in isolation; a synagogue that successfully retains its members over time begins with a recruitment campaign, follows with a program of new member integration, and then continues with various programs to aid in membership retention. Improving temple membership is a *process,* and there is no list of programs that one can simply implement in place of that process.

The issues surrounding temple membership touch upon all aspects of congregational life and far surpass the work of the membership committee alone. To be most successful, the process of membership recruitment, integration and retention must begin with an examination of the fundamentals of congregational identity and essential purpose. Until a congregation can clearly define its identity — the values and beliefs for which it stands, the style that makes it distinctive — reaching out to others cannot have maximum impact. When a congregation knows who it is, what makes it unique, and why it exists, it can succesfully motivate more of its members to become involved and to explore ways in which they can encourage others who believe similarly to join. Once a congregation operates efficiently, making the most of its human and financial resources, once congregants are trained appropriately for positions they undertake and are acknowledged properly for their efforts, and once all congregational activities are grounded in the mission of a Reform Jewish congregation, then more congregants will become actively involved and maintain their memberships.

In order to assist congregations in the important task of building membership and reaching out to the unaffiliated, we have developed this resource of exercises and programmatic suggestions for membership recruitment, integration and retention. This book is intended for congregations of all sizes. We have tried to include suggestions and ideas for small, medium and large congregations alike. Where possible, we have indicated when a specific program or idea works best with congregations of a specific size, or how it might be adapted for other larger or smaller synagogues. Nonetheless, small, medium and large congregations do function differently, particularly in the areas of membership recruitment, integration and retention. The summary on "Congregational Responses: Different Size, Different Style" that follows may be helpful in understanding how your congregation functions as a result of its size.

USING THIS RESOURCE

This idea book has been created to help congregations build their membership through recruitment, integration and retention. Because we believe that this is a process and not a matter of programmatic suggestions alone, we have developed exercises for temple Boards of Directors and membership committees in addition to compiling lists of more practical suggestions for recruitment, integration and retention.

Chapter 1. Board Exercises is designed as a road map for congregations to follow, moving step-by-step from the basics of defining congregational identity and formulating a mission statement to annual evaluation exercises on progress. Congregations can plug into the book at the point most relevant for them, depending upon how far along they are already. When using these exercises, it is important to consider *all* temple activities; the term "congregation" includes the auxilaries, as well as all of the various temple committees. While designed primarily for the Board of Directors of a congregation, most of these exercises can also be used by individual committees or auxilaries, to help them evaluate their own activities as well as the way in which they fit in to the congregation as a whole.

The section opens with a sample of thought pieces that can be used as "ice-breakers" when introducing this process of self-evaluation and self-definition to the board. The rating scale, "Fulfilling our Purpose" is a good beginning piece for all congregations in that it is an extensive exercise that rates all major aspects of congregational life. As a beginning piece, it will help congregations focus on specific areas that need attention and set priorities; it can also be used on an on-going basis to evaluate progress and note changes over time. The next exercise, "Mission Statement, Goals and Objectives" will help congregations complete the basic steps of writing a mission statement and setting the goals and objectives that flow from that statement. The last two exercises in this section are tools to help congregations evaluate their progress in reaching their goals and focus on areas needing change.

Chapter 2. Membership Activities Assessment is designed for membership committees and/or Boards of Directors to use in evaluating their congregation's activities in the specific areas of membership recruitment, integration and retention. These exercises will help congregations take a fresh look at themselves and will lead to the development of appropriate responses to attract and keep more members.

Chapter 3. Practical Steps to Change offers a variety of programmatic ideas, working models, and tools for improving membership recruitment (including advertising and public relations tips), integration and retention. The programmatic ideas are given as *suggested* responses only; they are meant to stimulate the creation of responses which will fit the unique identity of each synagogue. While some of the ideas may be a perfect fit, others will need to be adapted. If you have questions about a specific program, please contact the congregation listed directly.

This idea book is the first major publication of the Task Force on the Unaffiliated. By no means is it complete. It is also the beginning of a process. Your feedback would be most appreciated. The ideas listed in the program sections do not represent all of the programs that are out there, only those about which we have learned. Please share with us your successful program ideas, so that we can pass them on to others in future supplements to this book and in our on-going communications with congregations. We learn the most by learning from one another. Please send your comments and program descriptions to:

Rabbi Renni S. Altman
UAHC Task Force on the Unaffiliated
838 Fifth Avenue
New York, NY 10021-7064

THE UNAFFILIATED

WHO ARE THEY?

The unaffiliated are the fastest growing segment of the Jewish population today. They are our family, friends, neighbors and business associates. They are young and old, married and single, gay and straight, parents and children. The Jewish family has undergone tremendous changes in the last few decades. Today, only *one in four* Jewish households, at the most, meets the definition of the "traditional Jewish family" (i.e., husband and wife, both of Jewish birth, who were never married previously, with two or more of their natural children). In order to meet the needs of the Jews of today, synagogue programming must respond to the realities of Jewish life and the changing definition of family.

The two most substantial and growing segments of the unaffiliated population are the intermarried and singles. The intermarried population is the least likely to affiliate, and they are the fastest growing segment of those 15% of the Jewish population who never affiliate. Being single today is an "official stage" of life, no longer a transition period between college and marriage. In fact, more people are spending a longer period in their life single than married. If congregations want to reach out to these two major populations of unaffiliated Jews, they will need to alter attitudes and develop programmatic responses to welcome intermarried families and single Jews.

WHY ARE THEY UNAFFILIATED?

In a study of the Dallas Jewish community, conducted by Dr. Tobin, the following reasons, in order of popularity, were given by unaffiliated Jews for not joining synagogues:

1. Other (don't like the rabbi, synagogue too far away, etc.)
2. High cost
3. "I'm not religious"/"I'm uncomfortable in services"
4. "There is nothing there for me"

These reasons for non-affiliation, particularly the last three, can serve as guidelines for congregations to follow in developing appropriate responses, both in policy and in programming to attract the unaffiliated.

A variety of other factors, which may be beyond the control of synagogues, also affect affiliation rates and should be taken into consideration in membership activities. Geographic location has a strong influence, for example. Rates of affiliation are generally high in the Midwest and low in the West and Sunbelt, areas to which Jews are relocating in droves. Increasing mobility negatively affects affiliation as the intergenerational bonds that once kept families in synagogues are broken and individuals are faced with the option of making new connections as adults. Today, one-half of the Jewish population in a given city was not born there. Migration to the outer suburbs of metropolitan areas also has a negative influence, as the Jews are generally too scattered, leaving no focal point around which a community can form. In addition, those who consider themselves Reform Jews or "just Jews" tend to affiliate less than those who consider themselves Conservative or Orthodox.

While certain factors, such as geographic location, are beyond a congregation's control, other factors influencing affiliation rates should be taken into account when designing ways to reach the unaffiliated. If people are moving away from their families, how can the synagogue become someone's extended family? Perhaps singles are not interested in Shabbat services, but what about Yom Kippur Break-Fast? Congregations can begin to reach out to the unaffiliated by learning first about the unaffiliated in their areas and then trying to respond to their needs.

CONGREGATIONAL RESPONSES: DIFFERENT SIZE, DIFFERENT STYLE

Size is one of the most influential factors in the way congregations choose to reach out to the unaffiliated. A congregation's personality, its ability to develop programs, its financial resources, the interactions between congregants — these factors are all affected by a congregation's size. A congregation's ability to successfully recruit, integrate and retain members is largely dependent upon its ability to recognize the limits that its size implies and to take advantage of the options that its size offers.

Following are some general statements regarding the nature of congregations of different sizes and ways in which size influences their membership activities. As these are generalizations, they may not apply to every congregation and characteristics of different sizes may overlap in your congregation as well.

Small Congregations (A, AB)

Small congregations are generally characterized by a family or "clan"-like nature in which members feel strongly bonded to one another. They like the congregation particularly for its small size and tend to value their relationships within the congregation more highly than particular programs. Individuals will tend naturally to assume different roles, such as that of the critic, the "gatekeeper" (greeter of new people), and the matriarch or patriarch (informal head of the congregation). While a newcomer will readily become well-known within this "family", as with all families, acceptance as an "insider" will not occur until all members have gotten to know the newcomer and the matriarch or patriarch gives his or her stamp of approval. Often the rabbi of a small congregation serves on a part-time basis or else is not with the congregation for a long time. Therefore, while the rabbi plays an important role in welcoming newcomers, it is the acceptance of other *members* that is most important.

Medium Congregations (B,C)

In medium conngregations, already too large to be a single community, smaller groups form around specific programmatic interests and committees, each of which may function like a clan or family. Because of the diversity of groups and activities, one experiences less unity within a medium-sized congregation than in a smaller one. Instead of a matriarch or patriarch in the leadership position, a mid-sized congregation is generally run by a leadership circle, led by the rabbi. The congregation is structured like a wheel, with the rabbi at the hub, directly involved in everything. Newcomers to the congregation will generally first bond with the rabbi and only then with the laity. While newcomers to all congregations will expect a certain amount of attention from the rabbi, newcomers to medium-sized congregations will expect more attention. Because the rabbi of a medium congregation devotes much energy to the recruitment of each new member, there will be a limited number of newcomers to the congregation unless the laity also gets actively involved in membership recruitment. A partnership between the rabbi and the lay leadership is vital for successfully integrating new members. In comparison with a small congregation, it is much easier for a newcomer to feel a part of the general congregational community, but still difficult to break into the leadership circle.

Large Congregations (C-E)

There are many centers of activity in large congregations and representatives of different committees do most of the work of directing the synagogue. The rabbi(s) of a large congregation cannot be directly involved in all levels of temple activity and spends more time delegating responsibilities and in training and management activities with a leadership group, and less time in direct contact with individual congregants and newcomers. Unlike the experience in smaller congregations, newcomers to a large congregation will enter a specific subgroup rather than becoming part of the whole. When newcomers demonstrate leadership potential while in a New Member Class, a committee or another subgroup, they may be tapped for a leadership position and brought into the active center of the congregation. However, the anonymity of a large congregation makes it very easy for newcomers to get lost; if they are not self-motivated to become insiders, most often they will not get involved. As newcomers most likely do not expect the senior rabbi to introduce them and bring them into temple life, the role of the lay leadership in integrating new members becomes that much more important.

CHAPTER 1

BOARD EXERCISES

This chapter is designed as a road map for congregations to follow, enabling them to move step-by-step from the basics of defining congregational identity and formulating a mission statement to annual evaluations on progress. Congregations can enter the process at the point most relevant for them, depending upon how far along they are already.

HOW TO BEGIN: THOUGHT PIECES

In order to set an appropriate tone for your session using the materials in this book, you might begin with one of the thought pieces that follow. Their purpose is to help focus attention on the essential issues you wish to discuss: the purpose and nature of your temple.

You can use these thought pieces in any number of formats:

1. *D'var Torah (a short teaching from Torah):* By beginning a Board meeting with a *d'var Torah,* you can set a tone for the meeting which moves it beyond a management session. A *d'var Torah,* aside from being a wonderful opportunity to teach and learn Torah, also serves as a reminder that activities in the temple evolve out of a commitment to Torah and Judaism. In addition, writing *divrei Torah* offers lay leaders the experience of grappling with the text themselves and forming their own personal connections to Torah.

While traditionally a *d'var Torah* can be simply an application of a teaching in the weekly *parasha* (Torah reading), it does not need to be limited to a reading from Torah in the literal sense of the word; Torah can also be understood in a broader context to include all Jewish teachings. Thus, you might incorporate any of the pieces that follow into a *d'var Torah* in which you interpret the piece and connect it to your work as a Temple Board.

2. *Discussion Ice-Breakers:* You can also use these thought pieces as a vehicle to begin a short discussion prior to using the exercises in the book. The goal of such a discussion is not to elucidate a list of programs that the synagogue has or should have to respond to the issues raised in the thought piece; rather, the goal is to discuss the nature and purpose of your synagogue and your role as members of its Board of Directors. Select a piece, or combination of pieces, and duplicate it for everyone. Invite someone to read the piece aloud. Initiate discussion with the suggested questions that follow each piece.

Creating a Welcoming Congregation

1. One who has not seen the synagogue in Alexandria has not seen the glory of Israel. The congregation did not sit together without plan, but in guilds: the goldsmiths in one section; the silversmiths in another, each group separate from its fellows. When a poor craftsman entered, he took his seat among the members of his guild who maintained him and assisted him in obtaining employment.

Babylonian Talmud,
Sukkah, 51b

Q. In what way does the seating arrangement represent "the glory of Israel"?

Q. While congregations are no longer divided into guilds, there are other divisions of membership (i.e., singles, elderly). Do these divisions exist within our congregation? If so, what are they?

Q. What are the benefits and/or disadvantages of these divisions for our congregation?

Q. How does this segregation affect a new person coming into the congregation?

Q. How would you feel entering the synagogue in Alexandria if you were not a member of a guild?

2. I come to the synagogue to probe my weakness and my strength, and to fill the gap between my profession and my practice. I come to lift myself by my bootstraps. I come to quiet the turbulence of my heart, restrain its mad impulsiveness and check the itching eagerness of my every muscle to outsmart and outdistance my neighbor. I come for self-renewal and regeneration. I come into the sadness and compassion permeating the synagogue to contemplate and be instructed.

Rabbi Solomon Goldman
Anshe Emeth Synagogue
Chicago, IL (1921 - 1953)

Q. Compare Goldman's view of the synagogue with the view of the synagogue of Alexandria.

Q. Does our synagogue foster regeneration, encourage contemplation and offer compassion? Should it?

Q. Why do you come to the synagogue?

UAHC Task Force on the Unaffiliated

3. Jews need one another, and therefore congregations, to do *primary religious acts* which they should not, and probably cannot, do alone. Doing primary religious acts is the only way we have of growing as Jews. Consequently, it is also the only justification for the existence of a congregation. Everything else congregations do, Jews can always do cheaper, easier, and better somewhere else.

> Rabbi Lawrence Kushner
> Congregation Beth El
> Sudbury, MA

Q. How would you define "primary religious acts"?

Q. How do you think Rabbi Kushner might respond to the vision of the synagogue in #1 and #2?

Q. Do you agree that activities that are not "primary religious acts" do not belong in the synagogue?

4. The synagogue historically has been fashioned to address the needs of Jews. If the synagogue as an institution is not doing that, then it is belying its true function to adapt to the community's needs. Individual Jews can effect change if rabbis and boards of trustees are sensitive to the diversity of needs within their communities and respond accordingly.

> Rabbi John Rosove
> Washington Hebrew Congregation,
> Washington, DC

Q. Do you agree with Rabbi Rosove's statement regarding the purpose of the synagogue? Why or why not?

Q. How does Rabbi Rosove's statement compare with that of Rabbi Kushner?

Q. In what ways should our synagogue respond to the diversity of needs of our members and/or of the Jewish community in our area who may not be members?

WHO ARE YOU?
DEFINING YOUR CONGREGATIONAL IDENTITY

Facilitator's Instructions

A congregation's identity — who you are, what you stand for, what makes you unqiue — is perhaps the most influential factor in all of your activities. A congregation's identity is expressed in its programs, in its worship services, in the way congregants interact with one another. Awareness of congregational identity, along with the ability to articulate that identity, is a crucial step in creating a vibrant congregation, one in which all aspects of congregational life are in harmony with one another.

Congregational identity is particularly important in the area of membership recruitment. It is difficult to invite people to join you if you cannot present a clear picture of the kind of congregation you are asking them to join.

Temple leaders, both Board members and those active in committees, should be able clearly to articulate a statement of the temple's unique identity. With that statement in mind, they can more effectively develop programs and conduct activities which are in consonance with that identity.

GOALS

1. To articulate a clear sense of the congregation's unique identity.
2. To learn about the different ways in which congregants' view their congregation

PROCEDURE

This exercise, which takes a minimum of 30 minutes, can be used at a Board retreat or as part of a Board meeting or within individual committee or auxilary meetings. Ideally, it should be used when a new Board comes into office or prior to the time when plans for a new year of programming and membership recruitment get underway.

Step 1.   Divide into groups of four to five people. Ask one person to serve as facilitator, to lead the group's discussion and take notes. Make sure that everyone has pencil and paper.

Step 2.   Ask everyone to imagine that they are inviting someone to join your temple. Write a short paragraph describing the temple to this person. Descriptions should answer the following questions:

* Who are we?

* What is important to us?

* What is our style? (e.g., Classical Reform, traditional, laid back, warm, etc.)

* What makes us unique?

* Why is being a member important to me?

Step 3.   Have everyone in each group share their descriptions and compare them. How are they similar? How do they differ? Ask particpants to cite specific ways in which the characteristics they stated manifest themselves (i.e., we are a more traditional congregation — we use a lot of Hebrew in the service and most congregants wear kippot).

Step 4.   In small groups, try to create one inclusive description.

Step 5.   Bring the groups together to share the different descriptions. Have the facilitators from the different groups present the major points in their discussions.

Step 6.   Publicize the different descriptions to the rest of the congregation through the temple bulletin or other vehicles and invite feedback.

** You might also consider using the descriptions as part of an advertising campaign.

FULFILLING OUR PURPOSE
A RATING SCALE OF CONGREGATIONAL ACTIVITIES

INTRODUCTION

The quality of life within a congregation has direct correlation to the retention of members. In a strong, vibrant congregation, the temple community exudes a sense of well-being that is reflected in its programs and services. The atmosphere in the congregation is usually upbeat, and the participation level is high. This kind of community tends to be welcoming, so new members are more easily attracted and integrated. Integration leads to commitment which leads to retention.

In order for a congregation to function well, all systems must be in harmony; they are all interdependent on each other. If your members are not integrated into the temple community, you will lack participation. Without leadership training, you will lack trained volunteers. If the lay leadership and the professional staff are not working as a team, there will not be a clear sense of direction. Good leadership provides good administration. Good administration provides clear communication. Clear communication invites participation. Active participation encourages ideas and programs. Quality programs involve more congregants. More involvement leads to more commitment, and the circle continues round and round.

As the president or as a leader of your congregation, the thought of examining all aspects of congregational life might be overwhelming; however, do not be daunted. Using the following self-assessment tool will help you begin a process that will enable you to obtain valuable information in a manageable way.

"Fulfilling Our Purpose" is a rating scale that examines a congregation's activities according to the synagogue's three essential purposes: a *BEIT T'FILLAH,* a house of prayer; a *BEIT MIDRASH,* a house of study; and a *BEIT KNESSET,* a house of assembly. By using this exercise, you will get a sense of the quality of life and the effectiveness of your service delivery as they are perceived by the respondents.

This rating scale, which only takes ten to fifteen minutes to fill out, can be used by a congregation in a multitude of ways. It can be used by a board, prior to writing a mission statement, to assist them as they focus on goals and objectives. It can also be used as an overall evaluative tool to determine the strengths and weaknesses of the congregation; and when a new board takes office, it can be used to set their direction, or at the end of a term, to evaluate how well they have done. The board can use this in one session or as part of an ongoing agenda, discussing sections or individual questions within the framework of regularly scheduled board meetings. Another option would be to divide the rating scale assigning the *"BEIT T'FILLAH"* section to the ritual committee, the *"BEIT MIDRASH"* section to the education committee (and adult education, if they are separate), and the *"BEIT KNESSET"* section to the appropriate committees; i.e., "The Synagogue as a Community" and "The Synagogue in the Larger Community" to social action, "Building Membership" to membership, "Finances" to the finance committee, with the remaining pieces on "Leadership - Organizational Management," "Attitudes" and "Affiliation in the Reform Movement" being assigned to the board. These sections can be discussed by the individual committees who then report back to the board with their findings along with any recommendations for action they feel would be appropriate. There is no right or wrong way to use this exercise. It will fit into each congregation differently. Your time constraints and needs will determine its usage.

As with any other exercise in this book, the emphasis needs to be on the process, not the answers per se. In this instance, process involves three steps:

1. *PERCEPTION*

   During the discussion, you will find one person has answered a question with a four, while another rated the same question, two. Who is right? Is the answer really three? Only by discussing each person's perception, can you get a sense of what is really happening.

2. *RELEVANCE*

   In many instances, you will need to discuss what is relevant to your congregation; i.e., is your congregation located in an area that has a larger Jewish community, and is it important to be involved in the work of that community; do you or should you provide open forums on social issues? Through the process of discussion, the sharing of ideas, feelings and individual expectations, you will be able to decide if something is right for your congregation.

3. *RESPONSES*

   Once you have determined what is happening and what is relevant, you need to develop the appropriate responses.

Focusing on the purposes of your congregation and examining the quality of congregational life will be a new experience for many congregational boards. This kind of thought process elevates the discussion far beyond the leaky roof or latest fundraiser. When you begin this process, you are empowering your board to function at the highest level and to make a difference in the future of your congregation.

FULFILLING OUR PURPOSE
A RATING SCALE OF CONGREGATIONAL ACTIVITIES
Facilitator's Instructions

GOALS

1. To enable congregations to assess the quality of congregational life within its various activities
2. To assist congregations as they focus on their purpose and set goals for their future
3. To enable a board to evaluate its programs and develop appropriate responses.

PROCEDURE

This exercise is designed to be used in a multitude of ways and at various times within a congregation. Your approach to it will have to be tailored to the group that is using it and the length of time allowed for the exercise. This can be used by a congregation prior to writing a mission statement for the express purpose of helping them to focus on the purposes of a synagogue and defining their own goals and objectives. As an evaluative tool, it can be used at any time to assess the quality of life, programs and services within the congregation. A board can use this as it begins its term to plan its agenda, and again, at the end of its tenure to evaluate how well it has done.

The most important part of this exercise is the process. It only takes ten to fifteen minutes to fill out the rating scale and about an hour for discussion. When discussing the entire scale, allow one to one and a half hours for the entire exercise.

There are three factors to be considered in your discussion: first, the perception of the respondent; second, the relevance of the issue to the congregation; third, the appropriate response.

STEP 1:

    A. Distribute copies of the rating scale.

    B. Ask the group to individually fill out the scale without discussion recording their perceptions (10-15 minutes).

    C. Caution them not to get stuck on any one question. They do not need the exact answer; you are looking for what they feel is the answer.

    D. Remind them that affiliate activities; i.e., Sisterhood, Brotherhood, etc., count when thinking about opportunities the congregation provides.

STEP 2: Take the rating scale a section at a time. First ask how everyone did on the section as a whole.

> How many scored good to excellent?
> How many scored fair to good?
> How many scored poor to fair?

Next, depending on the section, take one to three questions for discussion. First ask how everyone did on the question.

> How many scored a 4?
> How many scored a 3?
> How many scored a 2?
> How many scored a 1?

If there are various perceptions, ask someone why he/she rated this a four and someone else why he/she rated this a two. To provide further thought and discussion, ask questions about the question.

FOR EXAMPLE:

Section I: Question 1

We provide all segments of the congregation with opportunities for fulfilling worship experiences.

Questions:

What do we mean by segments of the congregation?
What are the segments of our congregation?
What opportunities do we provide?

Section II: A. "Adult Study" Question 3

A significant number of members participate in adult education regularly.

Questions:

What is significant? (50 to a congregation of 1000 families is quite different than to a congregation of 200 families.) Lead the discussion to get the group thinking about what is significant for them.

Section III: B. "The Synagogue in the Larger Community" Question 5

Temple members express a concern for and are active in social issues in our local community.

Questions:

What kind of social issues?
Is being active in the local community important to our congregation?
If so, why? If not, why not?

STEP 3:

A. Keep the group focused. The discussion should allow for the following:
   1. Sharing of ideas
   2. Sharing of feelings
   3. Individual expectations
   4. Group expectations
   5. Relevance to the congregation

B. Do not allow the group to spend too long on any one discussion. If you hit a major issue, suggest that they do one of the following:
   1. Set aside time at a future meeting to discuss it
   2. Send it to the appropriate committee for further discussion
   3. Create an ad hoc committee

SCORING:

Explain to the congregation that the scoring allows them to:
   A. Identify areas of strengths and weaknesses
   B. Prioritize their responses

IN SUMMATION:

Depending upon the use of the scale, whether it is an evaluation tool or a goal setting tool, the congregation should be reminded:
   A. Not to be overwhelmed by the process
   B. Small changes can make a big difference
   C. To prioritize their responses
   D. Rome was not built in a day

Fulfilling Our Purpose:
A Rating Scale of Congregational Activities

In the lists that follow, please rate each skill or quality on the line to its left, using numbers from one to four:

4 = Always
3 = Often
2 = Sometimes
1 = Rarely

The best way to complete this survey is to move through the form quickly, putting down the first number that comes to mind.

Do not get stymied on any particular section or question. What is important here is for you to record your perception.

I. The Synagogue is a **BEIT T'FILLAH**, a house of prayer.

1. ____ We provide all segments of the Congregation with opportunities for fulfilling worship experiences.
2. ____ A significant number of members attend worship services regularly.
3. ____ We provide a good balance of regular Shabbat services and creative worship opportunities.
4. ____ Members readily participate on the *Bimah* when asked.
5. ____ The Sermons and *Divrei Torah* given in our congregation enhance the worship experience.
6. ____ Musical aspects of our worship enable and encourage prayer.
7. ____ I feel that my need for prayer in the congregation is met.

II. The Synagogue is a **BEIT MIDRASH**, a house of study.

A. Adult Study

1. ____ Our congregation, including its affiliates, provides ample opportunities for the study of Torah.
2. ____ Study programs for adult members are inviting, well balanced, relevant and involving.
3. ____ A significant number of members participate in adult education regularly.
4. ____ Our congregation encourages and provides opportunities for families to learn together.
5. ____ Our Temple library is used frequently by members.
6. ____ I look to my congregation as a place of learning that stimulates my personal growth.

B. Religious Education for Children

1. ____ The religious education we provide for our children effectively fosters a positive Jewish identity.
2. ____ Curriculum is well balanced, relevant and involving.

☰ **UAHC Task Force on the Unaffiliated**

3. Teachers and staff in our religious school are:

      ____ Well trained

      ____ Committed to Judaism

      ____ Knowledgeable about Reform Judaism

      ____ Caring and supportive

      ____ Able to relate well with young people

4. ____ Our Rabbi(s) and Cantor are a strong presence in our religious school.

5. ____ Children in our school acquire the skills to participate actively in our worship services.

6. ____ Most children continue their formal education through Confirmation and/or high school.

7. ____ Parents share in their children's religious education by reinforcing it at home.

8. ____ Parents support the education programs for their children by volunteering and participating when invited.

III. The Synagogue is a **BEIT KNESSET**, a house of assembly.

A. The Synagogue as a Community

1. ____ We create a sense of community, caring and mutual concern within the congregation.

2. ____ Our congregation, as a community, fulfills the *mitzvot* of comforting the mourner, visiting the sick and welcoming the stranger.

3. ____ A significant number of congregants contribute to the building of community by choosing to participate in one or more of the following activities:

      Committees

      Membership in the auxiliaries

      Volunteering for special projects

      Supporting the activities of the auxiliaries and special interest groups

      Hosting the *Oneg Shabbat*

      Attending the annual meeting

4. ____ Our Congregation provides a variety of social opportunities that bring members together.

5. ____ Congregants contribute *tzedakah* to temple funds on a regular basis.

B. The Synagogue in the Larger Community

1. ____ Our members engage in a variety of congregation sponsored activities that foster *tikkun olam* (repair of the world).

2. ____ As a congregation, we participate in the activities of the larger Jewish community.

3. ____ Our congregation acts as an advocate for oppressed Jews throughout the world.

4. ____ Our congregation supports the State of Israel and is its advocate in the larger community.

5. ____ Temple members express a concern for and are active in social issues in our local community.

6. ____ Our congregation provides education and open forums on social issues.

7. ____ Our congregation participates in interfaith activities.

8. ____ Being part of my congregation motivates me to participate in *tikkun olam*.

C. Building Membership

1. ____ Our congregation creates a climate of acceptance and friendliness to the newcomer in the community.

2. ____ We have an active program to attract new members.

3. ____ We publicize our activities to let the wider community know what we are offering.

4. ____ I tell my friends what I like about our congregation and I invite them to come with me.

5. ____ Our building looks inviting and is easily accessible.

6. ____ The rabbi(s), cantor and/or congregants greet new people and provide follow up contact.

7. ____ We create opportunities to integrate new members into the congregation.

8. ____ We have an active Outreach Committee/Program and are sensitive to the needs of interfaith couples and Jews by choice.

9. ____ Our congregation is responsive to the diverse needs of our current and prospective multi-generational membership.

D. Leadership - Organizational Management

1. ____ The congregation makes wise use of its human resources, both lay and professional, prioritizing projects and distributing responsibility widely.

2. ____ We have an ongoing leadership development program that provides adequate training, support and supervision for responsible and challenging roles in the congregation.

3. ____ We have procedures in place for handling recurring situations so that our committees do not have to reinvent the process with each change in leadership.

4. ____ We conduct business efficiently in meetings while still paying attention to cooperative values and listening to those who want to speak.

5. ____ Committees function with clearly defined goals and objectives.

6. ____ Our congregation creatively and regularly shows its appreciation to volunteers who accept temple responsibility.

7. ____ Lay leaders and professional staff respect each other and work cooperatively.

8. ____ I am personally enriched by my involvement in the congregation.

E. Finances

1. ____ We allocate funds so that working budgets facilitate the programming priorities of the congregation.

2. ____ Budgeting allows for items which may not be practical necessities, but have aesthetic or human value.

3. ____ Fundraising efforts are not the major focus of congregational activity.

4. ____ Our fundraising efforts are well-organized and effective.

5. ____ We are sensitive to the different levels of financial support that members are capable of providing both in dues and in additional contributions.

F. Attitudes

1. ___ We exemplify the values and teachings of our Jewish heritage.
2. ___ We take pride in the work of this congregation and are committed to its future well-being *(L'dor Va'dor)*.
3. ___ We respect differences, especially the diversity of our membership.
4. ___ We remember to emphasize the positive by offering constructive feedback and giving credit for jobs well done.
5. ___ We encourage our members to express their feelings in appropriate ways, without being judgemental or inflexible.
6. ___ We cultivate enthusiasm and zest.
7. ___ We encourage congregants to maintain a sense of humor.

G. Affiliation in the Reform Movement

1. ___ We inform ourselves about the history and values of Reform Judaism.
2. ___ We keep in touch with current issues and developments in our movement.
3. We get involved as a congregation in:

       ___ Regional UAHC activities
       ___ National UAHC activities
       ___ We send our children to UAHC Camps

SCORING

I. The Synagogue as a *Beit T'Fillah.* Total: _____.

21 - 28	Good to Excellent
14 - 20	Fair to Good
7 - 13	Poor to Fair

II. The Synagogue as a *Beit Midrash.*

A. Adult Study. Total: _____.

18 - 24	Good to Excellent
12 - 17	Fair to Good
6 - 11	Poor to Fair

B. Religious Education for Children. Total: _____.

36 - 48	Good to Excellent
24 - 35	Fair to Good
12 - 23	Poor to Fair

III. The Synagogue as a *Beit Knesset.*

A. The Synagogue as a community. Total: _____.

15 - 20	Good to Excellent
10 - 14	Fair to Good
5 - 9	Poor to Fair

B. The Synagogue in the Larger Community. Total: _____.

24 - 32	Good to Excellent
16 - 23	Fair to Good
8 - 15	Poor to Fair

C. Building Membership. Total: _____.

27 - 36	Good to Excellent
18 - 26	Fair to Good
9 - 17	Poor to Fair

D. Leadership - Organizational Management. Total: _____.

24 - 32	Good to Excellent
16 - 23	Fair to Good
8 - 15	Poor to Fair

E. Finances. Total: _____.

15 - 20	Good to Excellent
10 - 14	Fair to Good
5 - 9	Poor to Fair

F. Attitudes. Total: _____.

21 - 28	Good to Excellent
14 - 20	Fair to Good
7 - 13	Poor to Fair

G. Affiliation in the Reform Movement. Total: _____.

15 - 20	Good to Excellent
10 - 14	Fair to Good
5 - 9	Poor to Fair

Grand Total on ALL Sections. Total: _____.

252 - 288	Excellent
216 - 251	Very Good
180 - 215	Fair to Good
144 - 179	Fair
108 - 143	Poor to Fair
72 - 107	Poor

Mission Statement, Goals and Objectives
"Who are we? Where are we going? How will we get there?"
Facilitator's Instructions

The process of defining a mission statement and setting temple goals and objectives is vital for a clear, common understanding of a synagogue's unique identity. Such an understanding, in turn, not only enables the temple to function well, it also contributes a sense of energy and purpose to efforts to recruit and integrate new members.

GOAL

To enable temple leadership to set policy and to program effectively by

1. Defining the mission or basic purpose of the congregation (Who are we?)
2. Identifying the goals of the congregation (Where are we going?)
3. Developing measurable objectives and actions for achieving temple goals (How will we get there?) Note: in larger congregations this goal might be accomplished by leadership supervision on the committee level.

Definitions:

A *mission statement* is a broad and general philosophical statement that expresses the most basic purpose of the temple. It answers the questions: "who are we and why are we engaged in this enterprise?"

> *Example:* "The purpose of this Congregation shall be to worship God in accordance with the faith of Judaism; to cultivate a love and understanding of the Jewish heritage; to stimulate fellowship in the Jewish Community; and to support the principles of righteousness and brotherhood in society at large." (Westchester Reform Temple, Scarsdale, NY)

Goals answer the question "where are we going?" and are closely related to the mission statement. They are long-range statements of what is to be accomplished, reflecting the norms, values and culture of the temple and engendering a common sense of purpose among congregants. Goals are typically very significant, general, and difficult to achieve; they can be an idealized outcome. They are not measurable.

> *Example:* To provide a wide variety of opportunities for Jewish learning for all temple members.

Objectives are specific statements of measured amounts of progress toward meeting goals. They answer the question "how will we get there?" Objectives should involve a stretch, but be *achievable* and *measurable*. An objective should have three components: quantity (how much), time (when) and outcome (what). Objectives provide the basis for evaluation of progress toward achievement of goals.

> *Example:* To increase adult education opportunities during the next two years by providing three different types of programs that will involve 35% of adult congregants.

> Action steps might then include scheduling beginning and advanced Hebrew classes, an adult Confirmation program and a biennial scholar-in-residence weekend.

PROCEDURE

Developing your temple's mission statement, goals and objectives is a process that can be completed either as part of a Board retreat or as a significant part of two successive Board meetings. It is accomplished in two stages: Part A, the formulation of a mission statement and related goals; and Part B, setting measurable objectives.

Part A: Developing a Mission Statement and Goals for Your Temple

Set the context for this activity by stating the importance of a mission statement and goals for effective leadership and planning. (You might review an existing mission statement as background.) This will be the first step in setting goals and objectives for the next fiscal year or program year.

Define mission statement, goals and objectives and state that you will initially be focusing on the first two: mission statement and goals. Emphasize the broad, general nature of both. Discussion of how goals will be accomplished, even whether they can be accomplished, is off limits in this part of the discussion.

Complete the following steps:

1. *Brainstorming.* In order to obtain the broadest range of ideas, ask everyone simply to offer their answers to the question, "What should our temple be?" Go around the circle as many times as needed, calling on each person in turn to express only one idea at a time until all ideas are exhausted. Participants may pass their turn. *Write down all ideas verbatim without debate.* Depending on the size of your Board, this can be done either with the entire group or in smaller groups. In either case, the list of ideas should be written so that all can see it—on a blackboard or on pieces of newsprint in front of the group.

2. *Categorizing.* Once you have gathered all of the suggestions, consolidate the lists into categories. Do not omit any suggestions. New lists of categories should be written down. (This may take place during a break.)

3. *Prioritizing.* Rank each idea or category as high, medium or low priority. While all of the ideas may be good ones, all of them do not necessarily belong in the mission statement or as overall goals of the temple. *Allow enough time for an extensive discussion at this point; you will be discussing the very essence of your congregation and outlining the future directions you want it to take.*

4. *Writing.* Once you reach a mutual consensus on the highest priorities to be included in your mission statement and temple goals, summarize the ideas for your mission statement in one or two concise paragraphs and list your goals. A sub-group from the Board might be appointed for this task. A draft should be submitted to the entire Board for comment. Once approved, the mission statement and goals can be disseminated throughout the entire congregation, perhaps through the temple bulletin, in membership materials, or in another appropriate manner.

5. *Using Your Mission Statement and Goals.* Once the mission statement and goals have been approved and publicized within the congregation, use them as a reference point. When decisions regarding temple policies and activities are made by the Board, committees and auxiliaries, they should be made with the mission statement and goals in mind. Is this decision in accord with our mission? Are we moving toward our goals? The mission statement and goals should be reviewed periodically, for instance when new leadership takes over, to determine is they are still an accurate portrayal of the purpose and goals of the temple.

<u>*Part B: Setting Measurable Objectives*</u>

The following activity can be done completely with the whole Board or small groups of Board members can each address a different goal. Alternatively, use one goal as an example of how to set objectives and actions as a way of training Board members and/or Committee chairpeople to set objectives and plan actions at the committee level.

Set the context by reminding Board members of the purpose of a mission statement and goals. As a broad statement of purpose, your mission statement and goals form the first step in what should be a three-part process:

1. Writing a mission statement and goals;

2. Setting measurable objectives for evaluating goal attainment; and

3. Creating actions that lead to fulfillment of objectives.

Following these three steps will enable your congregation to achieve its basic purpose.

Provide a copy of the mission statement and goals for each Board member. If you are doing the project as a whole group, complete the following steps:

1. For each goal, outline realistic, measurable objectives. Each goal may produce many different objectives. Create a hierarchy of priorities for objectives, so individuals or committees charged with carrying out the objectives will not be overwhelmed.

    a. Remember, objectives should be a stretch, but neverthess attainable.

    b. Objectives must be measurable and answer the questions "what, how much, when?"

2. Develop actions designed to meet the objectives. Be sure that particular individuals or committees are given responsibility for implementation.

If yours is a larger congregation with a well-developed committee structure, it is recommended that committees complete all of Part B and report to the Board on their progress. Since the committee will be charged with carrying out the objectives, committee members should have a voice in determining priorities and actions at this level.

Refer to the objectives created with this exercise on an annual basis as part of the temple's on-going evaluation of its progress toward reaching its goals. (See "Evaluating Progress" in this chapter.)

SAMPLE MISSION STATEMENTS

The purpose of this Temple and Jewish Community Center will be to maintain a place of religious workshop and to encourage religion and Jewish education, initiate and further Jewish family culture and activities; to cultivate a love and understanding of the Jewish heritage; to stimulate fellowship in the Jewish Community and to provide society an insight to our ways of life and beliefs.

> Temple Shalom Emeth
> Burlington, MA

... [T]o guard exclusively the heritage of Reform Judaism and to contribute to the education of its members and their families, the spiritual and cultural enrichment of their lives, their appreciation of their roles as good citizens and good Jews, and their responsibility and opportunity to help others, less favorably positioned, all within the scope of and the moral doctrines of Judaism;

> Indianapolis Hebrew Congregation
> Indianapolis, IN

The purposes of this congregation are to promote the enduring and fundamental principles of Judaism; to ensure the continuity of the Jewish people; to enable its adherents to develop a relationship to God through communal worship, study and assembly; and to apply the principles of Reform Judaism to the values and conduct of the individual, family and the society in which we live.

> Temple Sinai
> Rochester, NY

MISSION STATEMENT FOR TEMPLE SINAI

As adopted, November, 1991

STATEMENT OF PURPOSE:

Echoing the goals of its Founders, our congregation affirms the following as its purpose:

* to nurture a synagogue which shall be a Reform Jewish center dedicated to the study of Torah, the worship of God, and the gathering of our religious community

* to foster a living Reform Judaism in our synagogue and our homes as we seek to interpret the teachings and practices of our vast Tradition

* to encourage our members, by precept and example, to apply the teachings and practices of Reform Judaism to their daily lives so that we become instruments for perfecting the world

Specifically, we seek these key areas of results as indicators of our progress toward reaching the above goals. We want Temple Sinai to become a place:

1. that people WANT to come to and of which they are proud

2. in which the entire community is vital, growing and learning

3. in which people come to form a special connection to their religion and community: they treat it and each other with respect

4. that reaches out as well as in: where actively working to better the world is an essential part of being Jewish

The above is what we publish publicly; the following pages become the specific areas that the Board monitors regularly to assess our progress.

We see these goals, including the indicators, as being something that should be reviewed yearly by the board, by asking:

* Are these still our goals? If not, what are they?
* How are we doing in each of the measurable indicators?
* Do we need to modify the indicators themselves?
* What can we do differently to improve our performance?

KEY AREAS OF RESULTS WE WANT AND MEASURABLE INDICATORS:

GOAL	NOW	1 Year	5 Years	10 Years
1. Temple Sinai would be a place people WANT to come to and are proud of				
* Percent bringing guests to temple affairs (RABBI/RITUAL)	5	10	25	50
* Attendance increases at all functions				
Friday Services (RABBI/RITUAL)	55	75	150	250
Men's Club, Sisterhood functions (MEN'S, SISTERHOOD)	30	42	90	150
Participate in fund-raising events (FUND RAISING)	10%	20%	50%	100%
* Membership: lose fewer for reasons OTHER than moving away (MEMBERSHIP)	20?	15	10	0
2. The entire membership is a vital, growing, learning community				
Attendance level in school (SCHOOL ADMINISTRATOR)	80%	82%	90%	100%
Students stay in school after Bar/Bat Mitzvah: % confirmed	25%	30%	50%	100%

21

KEY AREAS OF RESULTS WE WANT AND MEASURABLE INDICATORS:

GOAL	NOW	1 Year	5 Years	10 Years
Ave. number young people at services (RABBI/RITUAL)	5	10	45	75
% Membership involved in adult education (ADULT ED)	10%	20%	50%	100%
Kids remain committed adults:				
% involved Judaically in college (RABBI? SCHOOL? SURVEY?)	9%			100%
Join a temple once working (SURVEY)	33%			100%
New ideas for programs, ritual improvements flow up from congregation (RITUAL)	3%	5%	25%	50%
3. The temple is a place that people come to to form a special connection to their religion, temple and community: they treat it and each other with respect				
Always can get a minyan when sit shivah (RITUAL)	?			100%
People reach out to others when ill: NO	41%			0

KEY AREAS OF RESULTS WE WANT AND MEASURABLE INDICATORS:

GOAL	NOW	1 Year	5 Years	10 Years
caring (SURVEY)				
Membership increases (MEMBERSHIP)	450 families	475	575	700
New members STAY: fewer drop outs (MEMBERSHIP)	?			100%
Always get sponsor for flowers, oneg: % sponsored (RITUAL)	?			100%
Less non religious behavior in temple: Ave # incidents (RABBI/RITUAL/USHERS)	?			0
Congregation is highly represented at each Bar Mitzvah (RABBI/RITUAL)	10%	14%	30%	50%
More Volunteerism: - % emergencies can get adequate volunteers (?RABBI?/OFFICE)	??%			100%
- % families help with Oneg prep (RITUAL/FACILITIES)	5%	10%	50%	100%
- # families active on committees (EACH COMMITTEE REPORTS)	100	150	300	500

23

KEY AREAS OF RESULTS WE WANT AND MEASURABLE INDICATORS:

GOAL	NOW	1 Year	5 Years	10 Years
4. We are a temple that reaches OUT as well as in: actively working to improve the world is a key part of our Judaism				
More Active Committee Members in Social Action (SOCIAL ACTION)	8	10	12	20
Active temple member participation in programs (SOCIAL ACTION)	100	200	500	1000
Financial support to Social Action causes: $'s raised (SOCIAL ACTION, OTHER ARMS)	??	??	??	??
The programs WORK: they define and meet their intended community goals (SOCIAL ACTION)	30%	40%	70%	100%
More intermarried families and Jews by choice attracted to temple programs and membership, or aided in desire to lead Jewish lives	??			
More coop. programs with other temples, churches and other community groups	2	3	5	10

(Temple Sinai, Sharon, MA)

EVALUATING PROGRESS

Facilitator's Instructions

On-going evaluation, at regular intervals, is the only way to judge if you are achieving your objectives, moving towards the goals you have set and keeping in line with your temple's Mission Statement. It is also crucial for proper program development and resource management. If you continue to strive towards reaching your overall goals and objectives, then you will also improve your ability to attract and retain members.

GOALS

1.   To evaluate the congregation's progress in reaching the goals and achieving the objectives that developed out of its Mission Statement.

2.   To take note of accomplishments in reaching goals and achieving objectives.

3.   To develop a realistic plan of action for as yet unfulfilled goals and objectives.

PROCEDURE

This exercise, which takes a minimum of one hour, is designed for temple Boards of Directors, committees and auxilaries as a tool for evaluating and planning temple activities. This is a follow-up exercise to "Mission Statement, Goals and Objectives" and should be conducted approximately one year following the creation of the Mission Statement and the outlining of goals and objectives, and at intervals of one year in ensuing years. Conduct this evaluation either towards the end of the temple's calendar year, so that you can plan appropriately for the coming year, or prior to the end of the budget year, so that you can allocate financial resources appropriately. Individual committees might want to conduct their evaluations prior to the Board's evaluation so that they could present their analysis to the Board for further discussion.

Step 1:   Provide participants with copies of the Mission Statement, goals and objectives and review them.

Step 2:   Accomplishments and Unfulfilled Goals and Objectives.

1.   Have participants *individually* list what they view as the temple's accomplishments over the last year in reaching the goals and objectives. Use the indicators you have established as guidelines.

2.   Have participants *individually* list what they view as the unfulfilled goals and objectives of the temple and suggested ways for meeting those goals and objectives in the future.

Step 3:   Compile separate lists of "Accomplishments" and "Unfulfilled Goals and Objectives" based on the participants' individual lists. Discuss the lists and examine carefully the list of "Unfulfilled Goals and Objectives". (Remember to include in your discussion the question, "are those goals still relevent?") Discuss the participants' suggestions for meeting those goals and develop a plan of action for implementation over the next year. Evaluate the resources that you have available to implement that plan; if need be, prioritize your objectives and allocate your resources accordingly.

Refer to the list throughout the year and set aside a specific time next year to re-evaluate the new plan of action.

(Adapted from Activity #31 in *A Facilitator Training Manual for Connecting Purpose, Process and People,* UAHC Commission on Synagogue Management Task Force on Leadership Development, Revised February, 1987)

Four Questions: Assets and Liabilities
Facilitator's Instructions

GOALS

1. To focus attention on personal strengths as a Jew.
2. To examine aspirations as a Jew.
3. To catalogue valued aspects of temple life which should be supported and fostered.
4. To identify areas of needed change in the temple.

PROCEDURE

This exercise, which requires 1 - 1 1/2 hours, is recommended for a temple Board of Directors, committees and/or auxiliaries. If used with the Board, divide Board members into smaller groups and reconvene at the conclusion of the exercise to share results. Using this exercise with temple committees and auxilaries as well will invite a broad range of opinions and suggestions. Once committees have completed the exercise, the results should be presented to the Board and discussed at a meeting. This exercise can be used to supplement the other evaluation exercises in this book.

The exercise is designed to enable congregants to evaluate their temple's ability to meet their personal needs as Jews. In order to do so, participants are first asked to clarify their own needs as Jews and then to determine what areas they would like to strengthen or change. They are then asked to evaluate their congregation as the place to meet those needs and to determine where improvements need to be made.

Because this exercise is based on personal needs and individual connections to the temple, it is very important, when introducing the exercise, to create a safe environment by reminding participants that this is not an evaluation of their needs, but of the temple's ability to respond to those needs. Participants should be true to their personal feelings as they write about the changes they would like to see in their own lives and in the temple.

Step 1: Allow approximately 10 minutes for writing responses to the four questions. Participants should write down their answers independently and without discussion.

Step 2: Ask participants to share their answers within the smaller groups, beginning with their personal needs and then their views on the assets and liabilities of the Temple. Instruct participants to listen to one another for understanding rather than entering into debate at this point. (The facilitator has the important role of guiding the nature of the discussion so that participants do not respond judgmentally to one another.)

Step 3: Have each group compile lists of the answers to Questions 3 and 4 and write them on newsprint. Discuss the lists and indicate which items the participants agree on and which represent diversity.

Step 4: The facilitators from each committee or subgroup should present their lists to the Board. Suggestions from the different lists should be combined and used for further discussion by the Board in determining the future direction of the temple. Analyze the suggestions in relationship with your temple's mission statement and the goals and objectives that were derived from it. Develop specific suggestions to continue to strengthen the assets listed as well as specific suggestions of changes to improve the liabilities discovered through this exercise.

(Adapted from Exercise 3.3 in *Reform Is A Verb,* by Leonard J. Fein, et. al., Long Range Planning Committee of the UAHC, 1972)

FOUR QUESTIONS: ASSETS AND LIABILITIES

The Four Questions are meant, as are the four questions in the Passover Seder, to provoke thought, discussion, awareness and concern about what is important to you and to your temple. Write your responses to each question in the space provided below.

1. What do I value most about my Jewishness?

2. What would I change to enrich my life as a Jew?

3. What is there about this congregation which enriches my life as a Jew?

4. What is there about this congregation which needs to be changed to enrich my life as a Jew?

CHAPTER 2

MEMBERSHIP ACTIVITIES ASSESSMENT

The exercises in this chapter are designed for membership committees and/or Boards of Directors to use in evaluating their congregation's activities in the specific areas of membership recruitment, integration and retention. These exercises will help congregations take a fresh look at themselves and will lead to the development of appropriate responses to attract and keep more members.

An "Open for Business" Inventory[*]

Many congregations believe that their buildings are open and welcoming. A closer look, however, shows that many obstacles often challenge visitors: locked doors, unmarked offices, poor lighting, and no posted schedules, to name just a few.

The following questionnaire has been devised to assist your Board of Trustees, your membership committee or your housing committee to evaluate how "open for business" your congregation really is.

		Yes	No
1.	Do you have an outdoor sign directing people to the temple office?	_____	_____
2.	Is the door leading to the office always unlocked during office hours?	_____	_____
3.	Once a person enters the building, is it obvious how to find the offices?	_____	_____
4.	Is the hallway leading to the office well-lit?	_____	_____
5.	Is your temple office open regular hours?	_____	_____
6.	Are your office hours posted?	_____	_____
7.	Is the rabbi normally available specific hours during the week?	_____	_____
8.	Do you have a comfortable waiting area for visitors to your temple office or for people waiting to see the rabbi?	_____	_____
9.	Does the person who answers your phone and receives your visitors, whether paid or volunteer, respond in a welcoming manner and make each caller and visitor feel like an important person, not an interruption?	_____	_____
10.	Has the person who answers your phone and receives visitors, whether paid or volunteer been trained to make referrals in crisis, whether the need is physical, emotional, or spiritual?	_____	_____

	Yes	No

11. a. Does your temple have a yellow
    pages listing? _____ _____

   b. If so, does it include driving directions
   or a map showing where the temple building is? _____ _____

   c. Does the ad list your temple's
   office hours? _____ _____

12. Are the names of the rabbi(s) and cantor
    listed on a prominent temple sign? _____ _____

13. Is a 24-hour emergency telephone number
    posted? _____ _____

14. Does the temple have a telephone answering
    service or answering machine that gives
    callers a number for emergencies? _____ _____

15. Do you hold both Shabbat evening and
    morning services? (Those who work may
    only be able to attend services at one
    of those times.) _____ _____

16. Do you offer more than one kind of worship
    service to attract different segments of
    your community? _____ _____

17. Do you have small groups intentionally
    structured to incorporate new people? _____ _____

18. Do you run a weekly ad in the religion
    section of your local newspaper? _____ _____

19. Do you place small but significant
    advertising in other sections of your
    local newspaper that tells about
    specialized services within your
    congregation (for example, a single
    parent support group)? _____ _____

20. Are the foyers of your building designed
    so people outside can see people inside,
    and thus know when you are "open for
    business"? _____ _____

Now, count your "yes" responses. If your temple's score is...

15-20	Your "OPEN" sign is shining bright!
10-15	You are usually open, but have room to improve.
6-10	Anyone determined enough can probably find you - eventually
0-5	Your temple may be your town's best kept secret.

The inventory is designed to measure how open for business your temple is under a variety of circumstances:

- Questions 1 through 10 reflect how available you are to a person not well-acquainted with your temple who comes to the office seeking help.

- Questions 9 through 14 indicate how well-prepared you are to respond to someone trying to reach you by telephone, particularly in a crisis.

- Questions 15 through 20 suggest how much effort your temple is making beyond the usual worship services to reach out to people who might attend programs open to the public.

Notice where most of your "yes" or "no" answers fall. To which of these three groups of people are you most available? Which are you least prepared to serve? Which "no" responses point to ways your temple could become more open for business?

* Adapted from THE CLERGY JOURNAL, March 1990 — Is Your Church Open For Business? by Ray Bowman and Eddy Hall. Copyright 1990 by Church Management, Inc., PO Box 162527, Austin, TX 78716. Used by permission.

NEW MEMBER RECRUITMENT AND INTEGRATION
ASSESSMENT SCALE

The following rating scale has been devised to assist your congregation in assessing its effectiveness in attracting and involving new members.

We recommend using it with your Board of Trustees or your Membership Committee. Plan to take two (2) hours, or at minimum, an hour and a half, for best results. When used with a group or committee, have each individual complete the survey independently first (10 minutes). Then have members share their responses to each question with the group. Allow the group to discuss each question in turn until a consensus is reached (but do not let failure to reach consensus on every question be a stumbling block; the discussion is the essential element).

The value of this process will be maximized by absolute candor and in-depth group discussion. For your congregation to increase its ability to incorporate members, your committee will first need to get a clear idea of your present process, with its strengths and weaknesses. A subsequent open discussion will then lead to practical solutions through which you may strengthen your congregation in areas where it is weak. Look to the Recruitment and Integration sections of Chapter 3 for suggested ways in which your congregation can improve your current efforts in these areas.

I. *Attracting/Recruiting*

1) Clergy and lay people in our congregation clearly articulate the values of God, Torah and Israel as expressed in Reform Judaism.

1	4	9	14	18
Untrue		Partially true		True

2) In our congregation our commitment to Torah is reflected in the way people relate to each other and by being a caring community.

1	4	9	14	18
Untrue		Partially true		True

3) I am pleased with the variety of ways our congregation attracts newcomers to the temple.

1	2	3	4	5
Untrue		Partially true		True

4) I am pleased with the positive image our congregation has in our community because of the various ways we serve it.

1	2	3	4	5
Untrue		Partially true		True

5) Our members regularly invite their unaffiliated friends and family members to attend our synagogue with them.

1	2	3	4	5
Untrue		Partially true		True

6) Add 2 points to your score for each of the following things you have going for you in attracting newcomers:

    _____   A parenting center / Daycare

    _____   Weekly newspaper, radio, TV ads

    _____   Attractive, easily-accessible buildings

    _____   Attractive, well-placed signs outside the temple that communicate times of services

    _____   Religious school

7) Add 2 points for every non-temple community group that uses your facilities on a regular basis, i.e. Boy Scout troop, AA, etc.

_____

_____

8) Our congregation easily recognizes visitors, and people go out of their way to make them feel accepted and welcome.

1	2	3	4	5
Untrue		Partially true		True

9) It is rare that a visitor leaves our congregation without someone getting a name and address for follow-up purposes.

1	2	3	4	5
Untrue		Partially true		True

10) Our congregation has an Oneg following Shabbat and festival services at which time visitors are approached warmly by members.

1	2	3	4	5
Untrue		Partially true		True

11) When it is obvious that visitors are lost in our congregation's liturgy, a member will offer to assist them to participate.

1	2	3	4	5
Untrue		Partially true		True

12) Give your congregation the prescribed points for each of the following:

    _____   Personal lay response to visitors in the *week* that follows their Shabbat attendance (9)

    _____   Personal lay response to visitors within a *month* of their attendance (5) (if you respond in a week, count these points too)

    _____   A staff member who makes calling on temple visitors a priority (9)

_____ A printed brochure/folder which describes the nature of our congregation and outlines temple programs offered. (5)

_____ A letter of welcome that is mailed to all visitors within a week (2)

_____ Babysitting provided during services in a clean, attractive area (5)

_____ Quality religious education for all ages (9)

_____ An active youth group (5)

_____ An active young adult group (ages 25-32) (5)

_____ An active couples group (5)

_____ An active retirees group (5)

_____ An active Sisterhood and/or Brotherhood (5)

_____ Torah study group (5)

_____ A variety of small groups (study, service, or committees) which are open to receiving newcomers (7)

_____ Periodic short orientation seminars for visitors assisting them to become familiar with the temple's liturgy, symbols, architecture (other than new member class) (9)

_____ A sheet or booklet in the pews of the transliterations of common prayers and songs that non-Hebrew readers can easily follow (2)

II. *Integration & Retention*

13) Our congregation requests all potential new members to attend new member classes of 2 sessions or more upon joining.

1	2	4	7	10
Untrue		Partially true		True

14) Our congregation makes clear to newcomers what is expected of them as members (eg. time and money).

1	2	4	7	10
Untrue		Partially true		True

15) Our congregation encourages new members to follow home observances such as Shabbat rituals.

1	2	3	4	5
Untrue		Partially true		True

16) Our congregation welcomes and recognizes new members during a special Shabbat service.

1	2	3	4	5
Untrue		Partially true		True

17) In addition to welcoming new members during a service, there is a special opportunity within the congregation to recognize new members and have them meet several other members, i.e. potluck dinner, luncheon with the rabbi, etc.

1	2	3	4	5
Untrue		Partially true		True

18) Our congregation assigns a buddy to new members to help introduce them into temple life.

1	2	3	4	5
Untrue		Partially true		True

19) Our congregation has a coordinator of lay volunteers or designated person(s) who interviews new members to ascertain

a) their skills and talents

1	2	3	4	5
Untrue		Partially true		True

b) their interests in specific temple activities

1	2	3	4	5
Untrue		Partially true		True

c) their desire for opportunities to expand their Jewish life through worship, study or the performance of mitzvot.

1	4	9	14	18
Untrue		Partially true		True

d) their commitment to opportunities for *tikkun olam* (repair of the world) and ways in which the temple can support their efforts (eg. social action).

1	4	9	14	18
Untrue		Partially true		True

20) Our congregation has a person who is sensitive to the involvement of lay volunteers, activating new people and ensuring prevention of burnout, (eg. watching for overuse of the same committed leaders.)

1	2	4	7	10
Untrue		Partially true		True

21) The membership committee is given the freedom to request all other committees in the temple to assist them in their task, eg. have property committee post better signs, train ushers in new member greeting, have music and worship committees more effectively gear services to newcomers, etc.

1	3	7	11	14
Untrue		Partially true		True

    I. Attracting/Recruiting   Total: _____ of possible 175

    II. Integration and Retention   Total: _____ of possible 111

                                Grand Total: _____

Good Score for a large temple:	240 or higher
Good Score for a mid-size temple:	210 or higher
Good Score for a small temple:	190 or higher
Fair Score for a large temple:	190 or higher
Fair Score for a mid-size temple:	165 or higher
Fair Score for a small temple:	150 or higher
Poor Score for a large temple:	189 or below
Poor Score for a mid-size temple:	164 or below
Poor Score for a small temple:	149 or below

9/91

EXPANDED INTEGRATION AND RETENTION ASSESSMENT SCALE

Many currently unaffiliated Jews were at one time members of congregations, but did not form lasting connections. This questionnaire is designed for congregational Boards and Membership Committees to assess their present process of integration and retention of members. Only by understanding the existing membership process can we begin to find ways to improve it.

Allow a minimum of 1 1/2 to 2 hours for this exercise. Ask each individual to complete the questionnaire independently first (10 minutes). Then have members share their individual responses to each question with the group. Discuss each question until a group consensus is reached. Ideas for improvement can be discussed for each question as well. While it is ideal for the group to reach consensus on every question, the discussion that the group enters into is even more important and ultimately, will generate ideas for ways in which your congregation can strengthen programs for integration and retention of members. Look to the Integration and Retention Sections in Chapter 3 for suggested ways in which your congregation can improve its efforts in these areas.

1. Our congregation requests all potential new members to attend new member classes of 2 sessions or more upon joining.

    | 1 | 2 | 3 | 4 | 5 | 6 |
    | Untrue | | Partially true | | Always true | |

2. Our congregation makes clear to newcomers what is expected of them as members.

    | 1 | 2 | 3 | 4 | 5 | 6 |
    | Untrue | | Partially true | | Always true | |

3. Our congregation assigns a buddy to new members to help introduce them into temple life.

    | 1 | 2 | 3 | 4 | 5 | 6 |
    | Untrue | | Partially true | | Always true | |

4. Our congregation welcomes and recognizes new members during a special Shabbat service.

    | 1 | 2 | 3 | 4 | 5 | 6 |
    | Untrue | | Partially true | | Always true | |

5. In addition to welcoming new members during a service, there is a special opportunity within the congregation to recognize new members and have them meet several other members, i.e. potluck dinner, luncheon with the rabbi, etc.

    | 1 | 2 | 3 | 4 | 5 | 6 |
    | Untrue | | Partially true | | Always true | |

6. Our congregation provides an opportunity for new members to meet and get to know one another.

    1   2   3   4   5   6
    Untrue   Partially true   Always true

7. Our congregation does a good job in matching the interests and abilities of members with the roles and tasks needed by the congregation.

    1   2   3   4   5   6
    Untrue   Partially true   Always true

8. Our congregation has a coordinator of lay volunteers or designated person(s) who interviews new members to ascertain

a) their skills and talents

    1   2   3   4   5   6
    Untrue   Partially true   Always true

b) their interests in specific temple activities

    1   2   3   4   5   6
    Untrue   Partially true   Always true

9. People receive adequate training for responsible and challenging roles in the congregation.

a) caring community or rabbi-assisting roles

    1   2   3   4   5   6
    Untrue   Partially true   Always true

b) committee chairs

    1   2   3   4   5   6
    Untrue   Partially true   Always true

c) officers of the congregation

    1   2   3   4   5   6
    Untrue   Partially true   Always true

10. Volunteers receive support and supervision in roles they assume in the congregation. (There is someone available to check on how they are doing or someone to whom they can turn should they run into difficulty.)

    1   2   3   4   5   6
    Untrue   Partially true   Always true

11. Our congregation periodically evaluates lay volunteers and gives them feedback on how they are doing in their assumed roles.

| 1 | 2 | 3 | 4 | 5 | 6 |
| Untrue | | Partially true | | Always true | |

12. Our congregation creatively and regularly shows its appreciation to volunteers who accept temple responsibility.

| 1 | 2 | 3 | 4 | 5 | 6 |
| Untrue | | Partially true | | Always true | |

13. Our congregation has a person who is sensitive to the involvement of lay volunteers, activating new people and ensuring prevention of burnout, (e.g. watching for overuse of the same committed leaders.)

| 1 | 2 | 3 | 4 | 5 | 6 |
| Untrue | | Partially true | | Always true | |

14. When volunteers experience some sort of crisis in their role, someone helps them with the situation immediately.

| 1 | 2 | 3 | 4 | 5 | 6 |
| Untrue | | Partially true | | Always true | |

15. Within 6 weeks of such a crisis, someone checks back with the volunteer to offer support and to be sure they are back on track.

| 1 | 2 | 3 | 4 | 5 | 6 |
| Untrue | | Partially true | | Always true | |

16. Our congregation encourages members to observe home rituals relating to Shabbat and holiday celebrations.

| 1 | 2 | 3 | 4 | 5 | 6 |
| Untrue | | Partially true | | Always true | |

17. Our congregation provides members with regular opportunities to expand their Jewish literacy and observance through worship, study and programs of tikkun olam, repair of the world.

| 1 | 2 | 3 | 4 | 5 | 6 |
| Untrue | | Partially true | | Always true | |

18. Opportunities for spiritual renewal are regularly offered to lay leaders who are deeply involved and may be overextended.

| 1 | 2 | 3 | 4 | 5 | 6 |
| Untrue | | Partially true | | Always true | |

Integration and Retention Rating Scale

Total Score: _____ of possible 126

Good Score for a large temple:	100 or higher
Good Score for a mid-size temple:	90 or higher
Good Score for a small temple:	80 or higher
Fair Score for a large temple:	90 or higher
Fair Score for a mid-size temple:	80 or higher
Fair Score for a small temple:	70 or higher
Poor Score for a large temple:	70 or lower
Poor Score for a mid-size temple:	65 or lower
Poor Score for a small temple:	60 or lower

9\91

CHAPTER 3

PRACTICAL STEPS TO CHANGE

A. RECRUITMENT

This section contains various suggestions and programmatic models to help congregations develop a successful plan for membership recruitment. There are suggestions for the membership committee, ways to attract new members, how to welcome visitors and steps for follow-up. In addition, there are separate sections on advertising and public relations, tools to sharpen recruitment skills and supplementary materials from congregations.

RECRUITMENT

Members are the life blood of congregations. New members revitalize congregations, bringing with them new energy, enthusiasm, commitment and ideas. They provide valuable reinforcements for volunteer activities and committees. New members also help to broaden the financial base of the congregation. Maintaining a steady stream of new members is vital for securing a congregation's future. The energies and resources devoted to membership recruitment are an investment in the temple's future.

Those synagogues that are most successful in attracting new members have congregants who are excited about their temple and communicate that excitement to their friends, relatives and others. A membership recruitment campaign is a great opportunity to revitalize the entire congregation and encourage everyone to become involved.

Many of the ideas and suggestions that follow in this chapter may seem self-evident to some, but perhaps those who have already accomplished some of the basic tasks of membership recruitment will discover new ideas as well.

I. THE MEMBERSHIP COMMITTEE

The membership committee has a vital role to play in the congregation in developing and implementing the nuts and bolts of the temple's membership campaign. A good membership committee can be the key to successful membership recruitment. Despite that fact, the membership committee is too often overlooked or relegated to a low level priority within the synagogue. The following are some suggestions for establishing a successful membership committee:

A. It should be composed of energetic individuals, who like working with people, who are genuinely committed to the future well-being of the congregation, and who believe the temple has something important to contribute to people's lives.

B. Its tasks should include the following:

1. discovering what is special about the temple and how to communicate that "special sense" to others

2. learning about the unaffiliated in the community — who they are, what their needs are

3. designing ways to attract new members, — working together with other temple committees in the process

4. meeting with potential members

5. following up with temple visitors and inquiries about the temple

6. helping to integrate new members into the life of the congregation

C. The membership committee will need the full support of the Board and the other committees in the temple. It must be understood throughout the congregation that recruitment is everyone's "job". Specifically, the membership committee needs adequate financial resources to support a well-designed membership campaign and the cooperation and involvement of all committees and auxilaries when called upon.

II. STEPS TO ATTRACTING NEW MEMBERS

A. Are you "Open for Business"? Is your temple accessible to the newcomer in your community? (See "Open For Business" Inventory in Chapter 2.) Implement the changes necessary to make your congregation more welcoming.

B. Find out why your new members joined and use that information as you strategize your membership campaign. (See the "New Member Poll" in this chapter.)

C. Develop appropriate ways of promoting your congregation in the community. (See Advertising section that follows.)

D. Actively seek out potential new members
* cull real estate lists for names of newcomers
* use school registration lists or condo newsletters to generate prospects lists
* contact Federation contributors

E. Create opportunities for potential members to learn about your congregation
* participate in community "Synagogue Fair" hosted by JCC or Federation (Chicago)
* participate in community-based "Synagogue Awareness Month" (Boston)
* sponsor your own Synagogue Fair and ask congregants to bring their friends (Wilshire Boulevard Temple, Los Angeles, CA)
* invite potential members to a series of open houses in the summer
* host parlor meetings in areas where there are potential members

F. Develop a program, appropriate to your congregation, which will also respond to the needs of the unaffiliated. Various temples have offered the following time-limited ways for prospective members to "test the waters":
* offer free family High Holy Day services open to the community (Peninsula Temple Beth El, San Mateo, CA)
* offer free kindergarten classes open to the community (Temple Beth El, Spring Valley, NY)
* open the religious school for a separate fee to non-members through the third grade
* open Tot Shabbat services to the community at no charge
* invite unaffiliated families to free holiday workshops
* create early childhood education programs, such as Mommy 'n Me, Cradle Roll, Holidays with Daddy, and open them to non-members. Have the temple's Young Couples Club invite parents of young children to join their activities (Temple Emeth, Teaneck, NJ)
* offer a series of "Doing Jewish" workshops that is open to the community at no charge, which covers topics such as Shabbat, Chanukah, Life-Cyle Events (Temple Emanu-El, Edison, NJ)
* offer a free "Lunch 'n Learn" class in your downtown area and invite non-members to participate (See Model program in this chapter)
* participate in the UAHC Privilege Card program by extending free memberships, reduced memberships or special privileges to young adults, age 22 -30. (Call UAHC Task Force on the Unaffiliated for more information.)
* create a young adults group open to non-members. The following are some examples:

    MATIV emphasizes social action by supporting a battered women's shelter and participating in other community activities. They have many social events and cultural events as well. (Temple Beth-El, Providence, RI)

Young Congregants meets for holiday celebrations, major social events and educational programs, including a one-day "Hebrew Marathon". A Young Congregants' Study Group meets on a regular basis with one of the rabbis and participates in an on-going dialogue with young black leaders. (Wilshire Boulevard Temple, Los Angeles, CA)

Young Adult Action Committee focuses on social action through hands-on activities and quarterly brunches. Members also participate in congregational activities such as the Purim Carnival and Yom Kippur Break-Fast. (Temple Emanuel, Dallas, TX)

* For Large Congregations: create a "Young Adults Congregation" within your temple; have special programs, worship services and family activities for the 35 and under crowd (Young Adults Congregation, Congregation Shaare Emeth, St. Louis, MO; Young People's Congregation, Fairmount Temple, Beachwood, OH; Junior Congregation, Rodeph Shalom Congregation, Pittsburg, PA; Temple Young Professionals, The Temple, Atlanta, GA; Young Adults Congregation, Congregation Rodeph Shalom, Philadelphia, PA).

G. Encourage *all* congregants to become involved in recruitment

* offer a training session for Board members and other active congregants on inviting their friends and neighbors to join (See "Invite a Friend" training exercise in this chapter)

* have the rabbi write a bulletin article urging all members to bring friends to temple

* sponsor a special "Invite a Friend" Shabbat and ask all members to bring their friends with them (Wilshire Boulevard Temple, Los Angeles, CA)

* offer members a discount on their dues if they bring in new members (Temple Emanu-El, Lynbrook, NY)

* conduct a one-day workshop on membership skills for the entire congregation to involve everyone in membership recruitment (Community Reform Temple, Westbury, NY)

H. The Cost Factor

The high cost of synagogue membership is one of the major factors deterring people from joining. While all congregations have real financial needs, a major portion of which is met by members' dues, congregations need to develop flexible dues structures in order to attract the unaffiliated:

* be very upfront with potential members about your dues relief process

* make your dues relief process a very "safe environment" in which potential members will not feel embarassed

* readily accept people's statements of what they cannot afford; do not ask for any proof such as tax statements

* develop alternative dues policies

— Congregation Shir Tikvah (Troy, MI) has a "Set Your Own Dues" category for those under 30 or over 65, with a minimum dues of the cost of High Holy Day tickets.

— Temple Kol Ami (Plantation, FL) has a "Set Your Own Dues" Policy for those under 30, which allows for free memberships.

* develop a step-by-step dues program where new members build up to full membership over their first few years in the congregation

* delay building fund pledges for the first three years of membership

> * use the description of special dues policies as an opportunity to explain the importance of synagogue dues and the responsibility that all in the community feel toward supporting this primary Jewish institution for the benefit of all.

III. WELCOMING VISITORS

By welcoming all visitors to your congregation and making them feel comfortable, you create a warm atmosphere which invites people to join. Since a Shabbat service is often the first experience that people have with your synagogue, it is important to make a good impression on newcomers at that time. It is also one of the few chances to obtain important information about potential members for follow-up. Try one of the following or create your own adaptation to suit your temple's style:

> * have clergy and representatives from the lay leadership form a receiving line *prior* to Shabbat services to welcome members and visitors as they enter the sanctuary (Temple Isaiah, Lexington, MA)
>
> * give visitors to services a rose for their lapel for easy identification.
>
> * give Board members large buttons saying "Ask Me About Temple X"
>
> * form a "Shalom Corps" of board members who, wearing identifying badges, arrive before services and stay afterwards to talk with visitors (Monmouth Reform Temple, Tinton Falls, NJ)
>
> * invite visitors to stand and introduce themselves following the kiddush
>
> * invite visitors to a designated "Shabbat Shalom" table hosted by a temple member at the Oneg Shabbat
>
> * ENCOURAGE ALL MEMBERS TO WELCOME VISITORS AND INTRODUCE THEMSELVES
>
> * ask ushers to offer latecomers a prayerbook open to the current page
>
> * use a visitor's sign-in book
>
> * leave cards in the pews for visitors to fill in and drop off
>
> * send potential members bulletins of activities for a minimum of 6 months (12 months would be ideal and even more effective)

IV. FOLLOW-UP

After someone has visited your synagogue or expressed an interest in the congregation, follow-up is vital. The following are suggested steps to take:

1. Make a follow-up phone call inquiring as to the person's experience at services, inviting them to services or a program, etc.

2. Find out what areas of congregational life s/he would be interested in and have a person with similar interests, or in a similar age or lifestyle category, contact them. You want potential members to feel that they will easily discover their "nitch" within the congregation. The second caller should emphasize the strengths of the temple and why s/he is a member.

   Temple Rodeph Torah of Western Monmouth (Marlboro, NJ) asks its new members to make the follow-up phone calls with potential members. New members can easily share their experiences in joining the synagogue.

3. Send the potential member an information packet about the temple which might include

* letters from the rabbi and president

* a temple brochure

* a temple calendar

* temple bulletins

* adult education flyer

* Outreach information

* religious school information

* dues information.

4. Make a follow-up phone call one to two weeks after the packet is sent and invite the potential member to services or a program, depending on his/her interests. Always offer to meet the person at the temple or, if possible, to pick the person up. If the person is not interested in a particular program, you might invite the person to your home or to meet somewhere for a meal to discuss the temple further.

5. Asking a potential member to join is perhaps the most difficult part of membership recruitment. (See "Invite a Friend" training exercise in this chapter.) REMEMBER, NEVER BE PUSHY. Always try to open the door and leave someone with positive feelings about the temple. If they are not ready to join at this time, they may be in the future. AVOID THE HARD SELL. Leave them with the message, "We'd love to have you join us."

6. Follow up on past prospects by some form of contact about every six months. Send a packet with a personalized letter encouraging them to come to temple again, recent bulletins, calendar, special programs, etc.

ADVERTISING YOUR CONGREGATION

In the days when there was one shul in a neighborhood, the idea that a synagogue would need to advertise in order to attract members was beyond imagination. Today, as we know, if a synagogue does not advertise, it could become a neighborhood's best kept secret. "But we can't afford to advertise", is a cry often heard from the temple's treasurer. Advertising, however, comes in many shapes and forms — and it does not have to cost a great deal to be effective. Good advertising does take time and effort, however, and a well thought out campaign. Remember always to ask new members and visitors how they heard about your temple so you can track the success of the advertising methods you choose.

Here are some tips to help you develop your temple's advertising strategy and some samples to get you started.

I. *PAID ADVERTISING*

The most expensive way to advertise your temple and its activities is through paid advertisements. The peak advertising period for temple membership is *mid-August through Rosh Hashanah* (unless Rosh Hashanah falls at the end of September, in which case you should begin advertising at the beginning of September). Unaffiliated Jews who are looking for a place to go for the Holy Days or who have children of religious school age are your target audience; now they are "ripe" for temple membership. If you have a small advertising budget, use it at this time. If you can afford more advertising during the year, spend the bulk of your budget on a pre-Holy Days media blitz.

By advertising *throughout the year* as well, you will continue to reach out to new residents in your community and other unaffiliated Jews who could be attracted to your temple at any time. Good opportunities to place advertisements would be for the festivals and holidays throughout the year (Sukkot, Chanukah, Passover), special temple events and programs (major speakers, holiday workshops, adult education), events for specific populations (young adults, families with young children, teenagers), etc.

A. NEWSPAPER ADVERTISING

Creating your ad

The first maxim of advertising is: *your ad can only be effective if people read it.* Your ad must grab people's attention; it must stand out on the page. Your ad should also reflect the personality of your congregation and set a tone that lets the reader know who you are.

Be *creative* in your concept and in your overall design. People will notice your ad and remember it!

> *Headlines* are your first opportunity to grab attention. Be clever, draw the person into the ad. Keep ads simple and concise. Use bold, clear print to help them stand out.
>
> Examples for the High Holy Days:
>
> > SOME PEOPLE JOIN A TEMPLE FOR THEIR CHILDREN.
> > OTHERS JOIN FOR THEMSELVES.
> >
> > JOINING TEMPLE BETH AM BRINGS YOU MORE THAN SEATS FOR
> > THE HIGH HOLY DAYS
> >
> > THERE'S A GROUP OF FRIENDLY NEIGHBORS
> > AT TEMPLE EMANUEL
> >
> > ARE YOUR CHILDREN READY FOR RELIGIOUS SCHOOL?
> > LET US TELL YOU ABOUT OURS
>
> *Artwork* - use Jewish symbols to let the reader know immediately that this is something Jewish (i.e., Star of David, shofar, Chanukah menorah). Borders or a bold outline will help the ad stand out. Depending on its complexity, your Temple logo will help identify your ad.

Copy - keep it simple; don't overload the ad with too many words. Think of who the ad is speaking to and use appropriate language and tone. Make sure that your words reflect your congregation's personality (especially that you are a Reform congregation). Provide just enough information to get readers interested and tell them how they can learn more. Always include the name of the congregation, address and phone number. If you are advertising a specific event, remember to include the day, date, time and place.

Consider creating a *series of ads* instead of repeating the same ad a number of times. Create an eye-catching format, but vary the headline and copy to target particular audiences, e.g. families with school-age children or interfaith couples.

Placing your ad

While you should always place your ads in the local Jewish newspaper, if there is one, remember that most of the unaffiliated (unless they are already actively seeking a temple to join) do *not* read the Jewish newspaper. In order to reach them, you should place your ads in the *local weekly paper* (a community paper, the Pennysaver, etc.) and in a *local daily paper.* In either paper, seek out the "religion" section (not the "church" section!) Submit your ads 7 - 10 days prior to the publication date. Papers have different deadlines, so remember to check with each one.

> *Daily paper* - most expensive, especially on Sunday which has the highest circulation. Ask your local salesperson which weekday edition would have feature articles of interest to your target audience and advertise in that section. (If Thursday is children's day, that might be a good choice for placing an ad geared to families with young children.)

> *Weekly paper* - request *far forward, right-hand page.* Since it is less expensive to advertise in a weekly, you will probably use it more often. Get to know the salesperson; it may help you get better advertising space.

B. YELLOW PAGES

Often overlooked, an ad in the yellow pages, especially with a map, is one of the best vehicles for on-going advertisement of your congregation.

C. RADIO COMMERCIALS

Radio is a good, but expensive, medium to use because many people listen. Pick a station that reaches your target audience:

* a general membership drive — what station reaches a cross-section of the population?

* a program for young adults — what station do they listen to?

Choose the time of day when the listenership is very high (mornings, early evening). In order for your message to get across on the radio you must repeat it frequently. If you cannot afford to do that, don't waste your money on running a commercial once a day. If you do choose radio, the radio station will help you and will have someone become the announcer. Submit your commercial four weeks prior to the desired date of the announcement.

Public service announcements (PSA): Radio stations are required to air a certain number of free announcements for community services and non-profit organizations. Although they are usually aired at times of low listenership, it couldn't hurt to submit a commercial as a PSA. Air the PSA four weeks prior to the event and ask the station manager to repeat it as often as possible. Contact your local radio station for the specifications on PSAs.

Radio stations often have "Community Bulletin Boards" where you can list times of upcoming events and special services. Contact your local radio station for more information.

Creating your commercial: As with newspaper ads, your commercial must grab people's attention from the opening. Keep it simple, as you do not have much time (30 - 60 seconds). This is one case where "less is better". Do not try to include *all* the virtues of your temple. Focus on one service or upcoming program. Repeat the pertinent information, name of the congregation, and the day, date, time and place of an event, throughout the commercial. Remember to give the phone number at the end and repeat it.

Sample commercial for the High Holy Days:

> "With the High Holy Days approaching, you're probably wondering where to go for Rosh Hashanah and Yom Kippur. If you're already a member of a temple, then you're set. If not, consider joining our congregation, (name of congregation) on (name of street, town).
>
> Come hear the shofar sound on Rosh Hashanah morning and the stirring call of Kol Nidrei on Yom Kippur eve. Bring your young children to our special services just for them and your teenager to our youth services.
>
> Come in to (temple name) and let's talk about membership. Call (phone number) or drop by. We're at (address).
>
> That phone number again: (repeat phone number)."

D. BROCHURES

An excellent vehicle for promoting your temple, especially among new residents, is by creating a brochure for placement with realtors and in public areas such as local government offices, civic centers, libraries and post offices. Simple, attractive brochures do not have to be expensive and will take only a one-time investment of time and creative energy to design. Like all advertising, the cover of the brochure should grab people's attention and have artwork which clearly identifies it as something Jewish. It can be a simple, fold-up piece that can stand in a display rack. Make sure that the copy or artwork at the top (that part that sticks up from the rack) clearly indicates the subject of the brochure. Describe the basic information about your temple and its programs in an inviting manner which encourages someone to inquire further. Place the pertinent contact information — name, address, phone — in a place of easy access in the brochure (i.e., back cover).

E. POSTERS

Posters are an inexpensive way to promote specific events around your community. Place posters in high traffic locations (civic centers, activity boards, shop windows) during peak membership season, prior to holidays throughout the year and before any special programs or events. Put up posters three to four weeks prior to the event.

Posters must grab people's attention and make them stop to read on:

* use colors that stand out — light colored paper with dark letters

* use creative headlines, in big, easy-to-read letters that stand out (see ad headlines for examples)

* use clear Jewish artwork

* use little additional copy, including only the basic information: the name of the event with day, date, time and place, name of congregation, address and phone number, cost if any (or indicate FREE)

II. FREE ADVERTISING

Whether or not you do any paid advertising, your temple should *always* take advantage of the opportunities for free advertising that exist in your community.

* list programs and events in the "community service" bulletins and announcements in local newspapers and on radio

* list your worship services in the local Jewish paper's worship directory and your activites in their calendar of events (i.e, list your singles activities in their singles calendar)

* list events in calendars published by the JCC and Federation

* find out if your town or city publishes a guide for new residents and include a description of your congregation

There are two other major sources of free advertising that are most effective and, more often than not, are overlooked by congregations: press releases and word-of-mouth.

A. PRESS RELEASES

In order for your congregation to be known in your community as "the temple to join", you have to tell others what is happening behind the temple doors. While advertising must be paid for, newspaper articles cost nothing. Newspaper editors are always looking for a different angle on an old story. You can send them a press release about a temple program or activity that will give them that angle. The major holidays, in particular, are occasions when editors are seeking out new ways to tell the holiday story. Also, any time your congregation is involved in service to the community (social action, interfaith programs), send in a press release.

The more press releases you send out, the better your chances are that news of your temple will reach the public. Remember, it is also good advertising for your congregation to be well known in the general community, beyond the boundaries of the Jewish community.

The following are some general guidelines for writing press releases:

Writing the Press Release

1. Type your press release on temple letterhead, double-spaced.

2. In the upper right corner, type and underline the words *"FOR IMMEDIATE RELEASE"* using capital letters and italics. If the information should be held for release on a specific date, then type *"FOR RELEASE ON (DATE)"*.

3. Just below that line, type the name, area code and telephone number of the person or persons to contact for further information.

4. Center, capitalize and underline the headline.

5. The first paragraph is indented and begins with the city and date. Thereafter, all paragraphs begin with an indented line.

6. In your release, answer the questions "Who, What, When, Where, Why and How." Strive to be clear and concise. Try to limit your information to one page, double-spaced.

7. If you must continue to a second page, type - more - on the bottom right side of the first page. The headline or abbreviated headline should then be typed on the upper left side of the second page, and type 2-2-2-2-2 across from the headline to the right side.

8. After typing the last line of information, skip to a few lines below and type the symbol -30-.

Sending out the Press Release

1. Send the press release to all newspapers, daily and weekly, in your area. To get the complete list of all newspapers, check your phone book and the reference section in your local library.

2. Try to send a black and white photo, not larger than 8x10, with your press release. Include an appropriate caption on the back or bottom of your photo. Try to use a photo that clearly shows the holiday or event you are publicizing, with key people in it. For example, to show a community Passover seder, send a picture of the rabbi with some congregants at a table with the various Passover symbols. Your photo and article have a better chance of being used if they include local people. Identify them on the back of the photo.

3. Send a cover letter with your press release and photo. It should be brief, stating the main point of the release, and that you are available if further information is required.

4. Send your press release to the following editors:

   Daily newspapers: Religion Editor, Lifestyle

   Editor, Community News Reporter

   Weekly Newspapers: Editor-in-Chief

   If you send information to more than one editor at a particular newspaper, copy the other editors on your cover letter.

5. Do make follow up phone calls, but don't nag. Wait a few days between phone calls. And don't call more than three times, unless you are specifically asked to call back. Be helpful to the editors and don't push too hard — you want them as your friends.

B. WORD OF MOUTH

Overall, the best advertisement you can have is the one-on-one of someone speaking positively about your congregation to a potential member. EVERY CONGREGANT IS YOUR TEMPLE'S BEST SALESPERSON. Encourage *all* of your members to talk about the temple and to invite their friends, neighbors and business associates to join them for services and temple programs. Nothing will influence a potential member more than hearing first-hand about a congregant's positive feelings about the temple and going to temple with them.

Word of mouth extends beyond your temple membership. Every article that appears in a newspaper about your temple, every time the rabbi appears on a radio talk show or television interview, every community or interfaith activity in which your temple is involved, spreads the word about your congregation. Each is like a stone cast in the water, sending out ever-widening circles around it. The more stones you cast, the more circles you create, and the more likely you are to attract potential members.

SIT.
STAND.
SIT.
STAND.
SIT.
STAND.
SIT.
STAND.
SIT.
STAND.
SIT.
STAND.
SIT.
STAND.
SIT.
STAND.

Sit down with us for Services on Friday night
and see what we stand for.
Fairmount Temple welcomes you to a
Prospective Members Reception,
July 12th. 7:15 p.m. Worship Service at 8:00.
23737 Fairmount Blvd. Beachwood. 464-1330.

ANSHE CHESED CONGREGATION
Fairmount Temple

55

WHO WAS IN THE SYNAGOGUE LAST WEEK?

- A young couple, along with family and friends, were celebrating the naming of their newborn daughter.
- A relocated engineer and his family were making Jewish connections with their new community.
- A lawyer who recently lost his father was saying Kaddish.
- A divorced mother and her sons were enjoying a children's Shabbat service.
- A real estate broker was learning Hebrew in preparation for her adult Bat Mitzvah.

Perhaps one of these persons was you. Perhaps one of these persons will be you.
Won't you help ensure that the synagogue will be there when one of these persons is you?

BE A PART– N·O·T A·P·A·R·T

The Synagogues of Needham and Dover Welcome You

Temple Aliyah
1664 Central Avenue, Needham (617) 444-8522
Elliot Schoenberg, Rabbi • Susan Karns, President

Temple Beth Shalom
670 Highland Avenue, Needham (617) 444-0077
Dr. Rifat Sonsino, Rabbi • Ina D. Glasberg, President

B'nai Jacob Synagogue
Donnelly Drive, Dover (508) 785-0990
Dr. Ira A. Korff, Rabbi • Neil Wolfman, President

THIS ADVERTISEMENT HAS BEEN PRODUCED BY THE SYNAGOGUE COUNCIL OF MASSACHUSETTS.
a joint venture of UAHC, United Synagogue, and Orthodox congregations in Massachusetts

---

A Family Place...

Our Congregation Proudly Offers:

Weekly Shabbat Services — We welcome you to join us
Friday evenings at 7:30 p.m.

Pre-School Programs (ages 2-5): "Club Yeladim" —
heritage oriented activities & "Tot Shabbat" —
monthly services geared for our youngest members

A Fully Accredited Religious School

Exciting Youth Group Activities

Men's Club/Women's Division

Enticing, Contemporary Adult School Activities

*From singles to "empty nesters," there is something
for everyone . . . We welcome your inquiry, please call*
Gale Brucker, Membership Chairperson — 580-0130
Rabbi Howard Jaffe — 356-8777

Mountain Jewish Community Center

104 MT. HOREB ROAD • WARREN, NEW JERSEY 07060
. . . a Place for Your Family

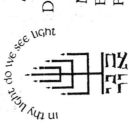

DO YOU MISS THE SOUND OF THE SHOFAR?

Ancient and mystical, the Shofar calls us to renewal on Rosh Hashanah and contemplation on Yom Kippur. Where will you hear the Shofar?

Why not with us? As a member of Temple Beth El, you're invited to all our High Holy Days observances PLUS a full year of Jewish cultural, social and educational activities. Discover the fulfillment available as a member of a vibrant Reform Jewish congregation.

For more information on membership and High Holy Day tickets, call us at 123-4567. L'Shanah Tovah – May you be inscribed for a good year!

TEMPLE BETH EL
100 TEMPLE WAY
TEMPLEVILLE, CE 10000

SAMPLE COPY FOR A PRE-HIGH HOLY DAY AD

GREET THE NEW YEAR WITH A NEW FAMILY THIS YEAR

With Rosh Hashanah arriving on (day, date), it's time to think "Temple".

Consider joining (Temple name) and become part of our family. We offer a full range of programs and services in a warm Reform Jewish setting: High Holy Day services; religious school; Sabbath and Festival services; year-round adult education programs and social activities.

Sounds like any Temple? Drop by and discover our special way of doing things.

Become part of our Jewish family.

(Temple name, address and phone number).

SAMPLE COPY FOR A POST-HIGH HOLY DAY AD

THERE'S MUCH MORE TO (TEMPLE NAME) THAN HIGH HOLY DAY SERVICES

We were glad to have so many people with us for the High Holy Days, but we hope you won't wait until next year to come back. At (Temple Name), we 've got a lot going on right now.

Religious school for the kids. Interesting continuing education for the adults. Enjoyable and contemporary Shabbat services for all. And many other social and cultural activities.

You're always welcome at (Temple name), but membership means you're part of our family.

Call (Temple number) and come visit.

(Temple name, address, phone number)

OUR PURIM BASH IS FOR CHILDREN OF ALL AGES

Children love Purim: the fun of shaking groggers to drown out Haman's name, the great party after the service. But Purim is not for children only – according to tradition, everyone should make Purim a wild celebration of Jewish freedom!

So why don't you join us? Our service starts on Monday, March 13 at 6:00pm, with a party following. Please call 123-4567 for reservations.

While you're on the phone, ask about membership in our congregation. We offer diversified cultural, educational and social programs for all ages. Let us show how much fun and fulfillment membership in a vibrant Reform Jewish congregation can offer.

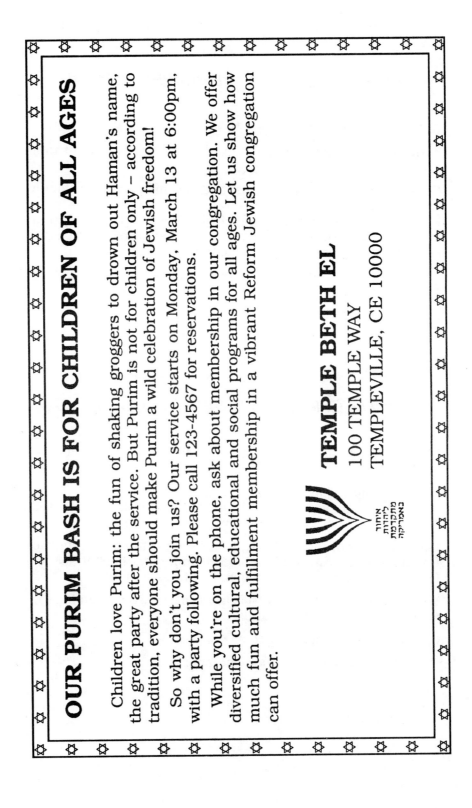

TEMPLE BETH EL
100 TEMPLE WAY
TEMPLEVILLE, CE 10000

BREAK MATZO WITH US

Moses didn't leave Israel alone – he probably left with one of *your* ancestors. Join us this year and relive their Exodus from Egypt.

Come to our congregation's seder on Monday, April 12 at 7:00p.m. Together let's celebrate our freedom from slavery and the continued vitality of the Jewish people.

While you're here, ask about membership in Temple Beth El. It's a great place to meet people, to make new friends. We offer many diversified cultural, social and educational programs. Let us show you how much fun and fulfillment membership in a Reform Jewish congregation can offer.

To make your seder reservations, or to get more information about our congregation, call us at 123-4567. And have a good Pesach!

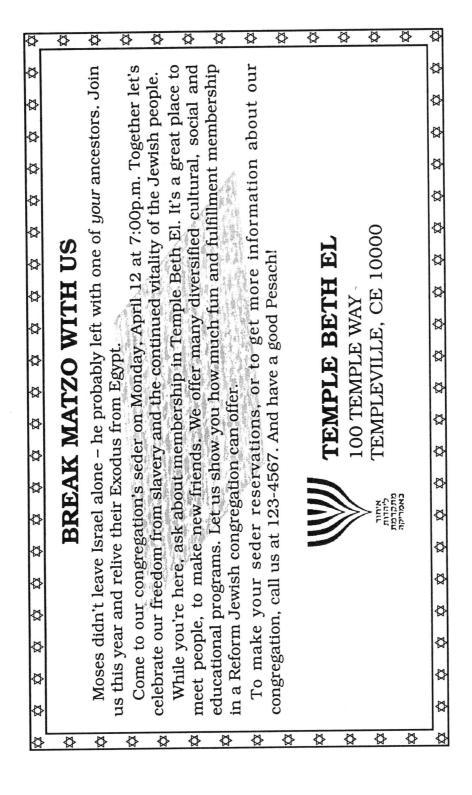

TEMPLE BETH EL

100 TEMPLE WAY -
TEMPLEVILLE, CE 10000

"Invite a Friend": A Training Exercise
Facilitator's Instructions

GOALS

1. To explore ways of inviting individuals and families to join congregations;

2. To see synagogue affiliation as a person-to-person process that requires listening, empathy and response to individual concerns;

3. To empower temple members to do the work of reaching out to unaffiliated Jews.

PROCEDURE

This exercise is designed for any group of temple members who are involved in recruitment. Most certainly, it can be used with Boards of Directors and membership committees, and as part of any temple program on membership.

The entire exercise, which centers around a role-play, requires a minimum of 45 minutes and can last one and a half hours, depending on the length of discussion.

Step 1:   Provide a brief introduction that includes the following points:

* Congregations need new members for many reasons. New members bring new ideas, energy and a broadened financial base.

* Congregations also have a responsibility to serve the variety of needs of the Jews in their communities for study, worship, social action and community.

* Often recruitment of new members is seen as the job of the Membership Committee. However, congregations that are most successful in attracting people have members who are excited about their synagogue and talk about it with their friends.

* Today, only 25 - 30% of the Jews in North America are affiliated with a synagogue; some three million Jews remain unaffiliated. They stay away because they view synagogue membership as too expensive, because they are uncomfortable in synagogues, and because they don't feel that synagogues offer them anything.

* The Jewish community has changed dramatically within the last decade — only approximately *one in four* households meets the definition of the traditional Jewish family (parents who are both born Jews and have never been married previously, with two or more children of their own). Synagogues are not in step with the changing demographics.

Step 2:   Introduce the role play by explaining that one of the best ways to understand the dynamics involved in asking people to join the temple — the feelings of the unaffiliated person as well as those of the temple member recruiting — is through role playing. In role playing, people "stand in the other person's shoes", by taking on the role of a person in a scenario and responding as they imagine their character would. Role playing enables us to learn to respond in more sensitive and helpful ways. There is no right or wrong way to act in a role play. Observers in the group watch the role play and later, with the participants, discuss how the characters interacted and the dynamics involved.

Step 3: Divide participants into groups of 6 or 7. Ask one person to act as director for each group to keep the group on track, assign roles as needed, help people to stay in role and lead discussion. The directors should ask for three people in each group to volunteer for the role play (or select three if no volunteers emerge), while the other participants act as observers.

Step 4: When the roles have been played out for 5-10 minutes, ask each of the observers to choose a role and step into it for another 5-10 minutes. Then discuss the role plays using the suggested questions that follow. A comparison of different approaches and different styles may be useful as well.

"Invite a Friend"

Setting the Scene: The Membership Committee of Temple Temple in a town near you has inaugurated a special membership recruitment campaign. Enlisting the help of the Board of Trustees and the entire temple membership, the Committee is hoping to increase the rate of affiliation in the area and bring the added vitality of new members to the temple. In this context Temple Temple member Michael (or Michelle) has decided to invite new neighbors David and Nancy, who have two small children, to join the temple.

Temple Member

You are a long-time member of Temple Temple, very active in the past, but now active only in the rabbi's study group and the annual Bazaar. Your children are grown and live in a nearby city, but have not joined a synagogue. Your congregation, Temple Temple, has initiated a membership recruitment drive and is encouraging all Temple Temple members to speak with their friends and neighbors about joining the congregation. You have new neighbors, David and Nancy, who recently moved in across the street, so you decide to give it a try. Your goal is to invite the couple to join.

David

You and your wife, Nancy, have recently moved to a new area with your toddler and newborn. You have a new job, new house and new baby. In your opinion, religion should be a private affair; organized religion only creates strife in the world. When you were growing up your family lived in a Jewish neighborhood, but never belonged to a synagogue.

Nancy

You and your husband, David, and two babies have recently moved to a new area. The neighborhood seems attractive and the neighbors have been friendly, but somewhat distant. You are hoping to get settled quickly and begin looking for a part-time job. You were raised and confirmed in a Reform temple which you visit when you visit your family. You expect that you will join a temple later when your children are ready for religious education.

"Invite a Friend"

Questions for discussion

1. Did the role play seem realistic? Why or why not?

2. Questions for Michael/Michelle: how does it feel to introduce the idea of joining the synagogue? Does it seem awkward? Why? What is the worst scenario you can imagine? How might you respond?

3. Questions for David and/or Nancy: How does it feel to be asked about temple membership? What about the invitation made you respond positively? Negatively? What other approaches might elicit a positive response?

4. List 5 ways to initiate an invitation for temple membership. List some funny ways. What about indirect approaches? Does an indirect approach set up a hidden agenda? What seems most comfortable to you? most effective? What kinds of "arguments" might be successful?

5. Does the generation gap between the inviter and invitee in the scenario affect the role play? How would your approach change if you were inviting someone at a similar life stage?

    Would your approach be different if you were inviting a young single person? a divorced man in his 40s? a person who has just retired and come to your community?

6. Who is on our "Membership Committees?" How can we engage a broad spectrum of total temple membership in this effort, rather than just the committee? What kind of training would be helpful?

Why Join Our Synagogue: A Focus Exercise

Facilitator's Instructions

In order to develeop a more effective program of recruitment, it is helpful for congregants to begin by first clarifying their own reasons for joining the temple when they did. Such an exercise will enable participants to make a more personal connection to the unaffiliated of today and to focus on their needs.

GOALS

1. To provide participants with a better understanding of the variety of reasons for affiliation.

2. To familiarize participants with the unaffiliated of today.

3. To consider ways in which the synagogue can become more responsive to the needs of the unaffiliated.

PROCEDURE

This exercise is designed to be used primarily by temple Boards of Directors and membership committees as a first step in planning a membership recruitment campaign. It will also be a helpful tool for temple auxilaries to use with regard to their own membership.

This exercise requires a minimum of *30 minutes* and could take up to an hour, depending upon the length of discussion.

1. Begin by telling the following story:

> Harry Golden used to tell a story about his father who, in his older years, began going to temple regularly with his friend, Mr. Goldstein.
>
> "Dad," the younger Golden said one day, "All these years you've told us you have been an avowed atheist, and now you go to temple with Goldstein almost every Shabbos. You don't believe in God! Why do you go?
>
> "Well, I'll tell you," came the reply. "Goldstein goes to temple to talk to God. *I* go to talk to Goldstein."

Re-enforce the message of the story: people go to and join synagogues for many different reasons, some of which are not at all apparent to the observer.

2. Ask participants to write down their answers to the following:

   1. List three reasons that you joined a synagogue when you originally became a member.
   2. List three reasons that you did not join the previous year.
   3. List three reasons that you are a member now.

3. Taking each question in turn, list the responses on a blackboard or newsprint pad. Group the responses where possible. Compare them to the following reasons that researchers have found for affiliation and non-affiliation:[*]

   (The statistics below provide a realistic view of the unaffiliated, which may be quite different from what people imagine.)

Primary Reasons for Joining a Synagogue
1. Education of children (32%)
2. Access to High Holy Day services (22%)
3. As Jews, we *should* belong (18%)
4. To make friends (16%)
5. Other family members belong (9%)

4. Compare the three different lists. Are they the same? How do they differ? How do participants feel their reasons compare with those who are joining temples today? Are there "good" and "bad" reasons for joining? How do those reasons change over time? Does the temple respond to those changes?

   How do participants feel about the reasons people are not joining temples today? How can we, as members of the temple board/membership committee, respond to those needs?

5. *Wrap up* with remarks about the spectrum of needs that synagogues fill, emphasizing the necessity to be careful in judging what is a "good" reason to join, seeing membership as an opportunity to deepen commitment. As people go through different stages of life, their needs change and so will their reasons for being part of a temple. If congregations want to retain their members over time, they need to be responsive to those changing needs. Regardless of members' reasons for joining when they did, congregations need to make their congregants' membership meaningful *today,* if they want them to remain part of the community *tomorrow.*

* From research in the Dallas Jewish Community conducted by Dr. Gary Tobin, Director of the Cohen Center for Modern Jewish Studies at Brandeis University

NEW MEMBER POLL

Instructions

Why do people join your temple? For the religious school? Because they like the rabbi? It's nearest their house? You're the only temple in town? According to a recent study of the Dallas Jewish Community, conducted by Dr. Gary Tobin, Directory of the Cohen Center for Modern Jewish Studies at Brandeis University, people joined synagogues for the following reasons:

Education of children	32%
Access to High Holy Day services	22%
As Jews, we *should* belong	18%
To make friends	16%
Other family members belong	9%

Knowing the reasons why people join *your* temple can tell you a great deal about yourselves. You can learn what it is that attracts people to your temple, what activities you already promote well and what you need to promote better. You can discover what your best kept secrets are, as well as the aspects of your congregation that don't work as well as you would like them to.

The new members in your temple are the best people to provide you with these insights. By including the attached New Member Poll in the membership packet that you give to each new member, you can learn their reasons for joining your temple. Ask them to complete it along with the membership application and intake form.

Since congregations generally attract the greatest number of new members right before the High Holy Days, use that time as an opportunity to evaluate the reasons why people join your temple. Have someone on the membership committee collect all of the New Member Polls and summarize the data. Present that information to the Board of Directors at their first meeting after the High Holy Days for discussion (you can simply fill out a blank New Member Poll with the totals from all of the forms). You might ask the following questions:

What surprises you about the responses?

What items do you think should be checked as "very important" that are not?

In response to the reasons selected as most important for the majority of the new members, what strengths of our temple might we focus on in our promotional advertising? Are there other strengths that would attract more people if they were promoted more fully?

What changes do you feel need to be made after learning about our new members' reasons for joining?

NEW MEMBER POLL

Welcome to (temple name)! We are very happy to have you as part of our congregational family. We are always looking for ways to improve our congregation so that it will continue to be a place that is warm and inviting to newcomers. Please take a few minutes to fill out this poll, indicating the reasons you joined our temple, so that we can continue to reach out to others.

	Very Important	Important	Not particularly Important
1. Close to where I/we live			
2. The religious school			
3. Like the rabbi			
4. Like the people who belong to this temple			
5. Good for my business			
6. Dues and fees less than other synagogues			
7. Attractive building			
8. Worship style most comfortable			
9. Reform ideology is what I believe in			
10. Friends belong			
11. Family belongs			
12. Other:			

_____

_____

Please circle the one reason which is the *most important reason* for you.

LUNCH 'N LEARN

Twice a month the rabbis of Temple Israel of Boston, MA bring Torah study into downtown Boston. Since many congregants find it difficult to come to temple either for an evening during the week or on the weekend, *but are interested in study,* the rabbis bring study to them in their place of business. Fourteen years ago, Rabbi Bernard Mehlman met with a group of congregants interested in adult education and proposed the idea of meeting over lunch in a downtown office building. Thus, "Lunch 'n Learn" was born and continues today with some 35 congregants meeting bi-monthly in downtown Boston for 12 months of the year. They have studied topics ranging from Maimonides' *Mishneh Torah* to Jewish prayer.

GOALS

1. To bring Jewish study to more Jews.

2. To enable congregants to participate in a temple activity near their workplace.

3. As a tool for recruitment, to attract non-members to the congregation.

For Recruitment Purposes: While "Lunch 'n Learn" is a wonderful program of adult education for congregants (and, therefore, will help in integration and retention of members), it can also be an excellent vehicle to reach non-members and attract them to your congregation. One would simply begin with a core group of congregants and ask them to invite their unaffiliated friends and business associates, and publicize the program in the community. When using "lunch 'n Learn" as a vehicle to attract new members, it is important to remember that the rabbi's time with the class is crucial for its success in attracting unaffiliated participants to your temple.

The following are some suggested steps to set up a "Lunch 'n Learn" program, based on the model of Temple Israel:

Getting Started

1. "Lunch 'n Learn" is not expensive to run. Participants pay for their own books and bring their own brown-bag lunch. Publicity is the only expense.

2. The rabbi meets with a few congregants interested in adult education who work in a central business area to propose the idea and obtain their support and participation.

3. Announce the program in the temple bulletin and spread by word of mouth (and if reaching out to the unaffiliated, also publicize it in the general community);

4. Arrange to meet in a conference or meeting room in an office building in a central business district. Look for a congregant who will offer to host the program in his/her office building without charge. If no such space is available, the temple will need to rent a meeting space.

5. Arrange a regular time to meet — i.e., first and third Monday, from 12:30 - 1:30. Supply coffee and tea; participants bring their own lunch, if they so choose.

6. Set the period of time during which the group will meet — i.e., October through May.

Running the Class

1. The first session should be an open planning session to discuss what participants want to study and to set the theme for the class.

2. Select the materials/books and order if necessary. Recommended beginning texts: *Pirke Avot; Hassidism and Modern Man,* by Martin Buber. If the group is predominantly of one profession (e.g., lawyers, business people), choose a relevant text (e.g. Talmud, Laws on business ethics).

3. While the rabbi/rabbis should *always* be present, the class is taught by the participants. (With multiple rabbis, there is always coverage in case one of the rabbis must be elsewhere. It is ideal if both rabbis can attend the class as much as possibile, so that there is always continuity.) The rabbi is there to serve as a facilitator for discussion, to help keep the group on track, as a resource in the class, and as an aid to participants when preparing their materials.

4. One or two participants take responsibility to teach a section or a chapter of the material. Allow the group to take as long as it needs to study each section or chapter before moving on. Obtain volunteers to teach the upcoming sections a few weeks in advance.

    Example: The original group from Temple Israel was comprised primarily of lawyers and they were interested in studying Jewish law. For 2-3 years they studied the *Mishneh Torah,* using a one-volume, Hebrew/English version. One or two people took responsibility for leading discussions on each part of the book.

5. The group then takes off on its own, choosing new topics when it is time to move on. The group from Temple Israel also chose to continue studying over the summer and now runs throughout the entire year. They moved on from <u>Mishneh Torah</u> to studying Rabbi Freehof's responsa for the Reform movement, Jewish prayer, *tzedakah,* liturgy and are now studying the book of Job.

Recommended Dos and Don'ts:

DO begin and end promptly! Participants are making the commitment to be there at the time selected; you must make the commitment to remain in that time frame.

DO maintain a serious tone about the class. Participants are giving up valuable business time to be there.

DO allow participants to take control of the class, so that it is *their* class. As facilitator, it is important that the rabbi keeps the group on track with the chosen topic.

DO keep the text shorter initially to set an inviting tone.

DO divide the texts into manageable sections so as not to overwhelm the person teaching.

DON'T allow the class to evolve into a party atmosphere by preoccupation with the food. Keep it simple by offering only coffee and tea; those who wish to bring lunch will do so. (The group may decide on its own to celebrate participants' birthdays in a small way or to mark the end of text with a small celebration.)

Community Reform Temple

712 THE PLAIN ROAD
WESTBURY, N.Y. 11590-5999
(516) 333-1839

28 Nisan 5750
April 23, 1990

Dear Congregant:

Will you rise to the challenge?

As I explained in my Rabbi's Message to you in this month's
Temple Times, involving and keeping our present members as
well as recruiting and involving new members are the best
ways to insure the stability of Community Reform Temple and
the future of the Jewish people.

The enclosed brochure describes the Membership and Marketing
Workshop which we will be holding on May 6th. Your
attendance at this workshop is essential to the success of
our membership drive.

The workshop offers you the opportunity to learn new skills
and to apply them for the benefit of our congregation. A
workshop like this would cost you anywhere from $75.00 to
$200.00 if it were offered in an industry or business
context. We are offering this workshop free of charge.
Our "profit" will be a financially stable and
programmatically vibrant congregation. This will take work.
It can also be lots of fun. Please sit down now, fill out
the registration form and return it to the temple. If you
will it and work for it, our congregation will flourish.

Rabbi Tarfon taught, "You are not required to complete the
work but neither are you at liberty to abstain from it."
                                        Pirke Avot 2.21

Looking forward to seeing you on May 6th...

בשלום ובברכה

Marc Gruber

וְעָשׂוּ לִי מִקְדָּשׁ וְשָׁכַנְתִּי בְּתוֹכָם (שְׁמוֹת כה ח)

LET THEM MAKE ME A SANCTUARY THAT I MAY DWELL AMONG THEM (EXODUS. 25 8)

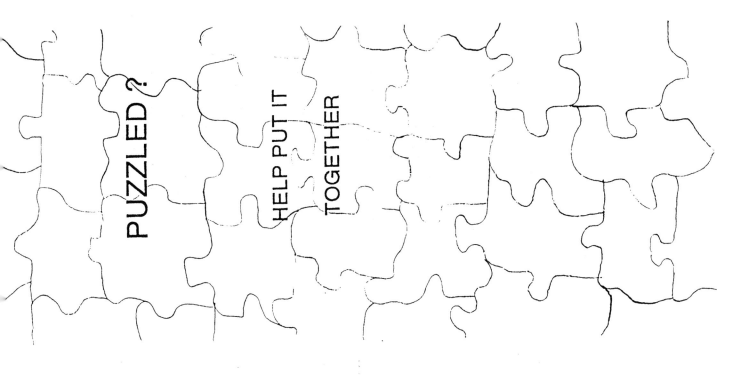

PUZZLED ?

HELP PUT IT

TOGETHER

WARMING UP THE CONGREGATION

1) Greet people you know, but spend time getting to know one or two people with whom you have never spoken.

2) Who breaks the ice? Odds are if you do not know who he or she is, he or she does not know you either. Be direct - ask for the person's name and give yours, get acquainted.

3) Watch for unfamiliar faces nursing a cup of coffee and looking lost. If you show interest in meeting newcomers, folks will think we are warm to "outsiders."

4) Tell a newcomer about various temple activities. This may be a challenge because you will have to find out first.

A friendly congregation is not a happenstance; it is your creation. Send folks away with a sermon in their minds and a song in their hearts and a desire to return soon.

REGISTRATION FORM

Yes, I will help piece the puzzle together!

Name: _____ Phone: _____

I wish to register for the following skills training session/work group.
Please pick a first and second choice.

___ Publicity ___ Tele-Marketing ___ Making the Sale ___ Integrating New Members ___ Retention

Please help me with child care. Names of child(ren) and age(s) _____

Questions? Please call Rabbi Marc A. Gruber at 333-1839.

Please return to: Community Reform Temple, 712 The Plain Road, Westbury, New York 11590.

75

A WORKSHOP
ON MEMBERSHIP AND MARKETING
FOR OUR CONGREGATION

SUNDAY, MAY 6TH, 1990

10:30 A.M. - 1:00 P.M.

COMMUNITY REFORM TEMPLE

Westbury, New York

PROGRAM

10:30 - 11:00 A.M.
Introduction & Keynote Address

Introduction - Rabbi Marc A. Gruber
Keynote - Mr. Larry Rothenberg

11:00 A.M. - 12:30 P.M.
Brunch and Work Groups

* *Publicity*

Skills Trainer - Mr. Robert Zimmerman
Coordinator - Ms. Ann Middleman

* *Tele-Marketing*

Skills Trainers - Mr. Herb Oster
  Ms. Lydia Oster
Coordinator - TBA

* *Making The Sale*

Skills Trainer - Mr. Robert Stein
Coordinator - Ms. Viki DeJong

* *Integrating New Members*

Skills Trainer - Mr. James E. Meyer
Coordinator - TBA

* *Retention*

Skills Trainer - Mr. Allan Mendels
Coordinator - Ms. Sue Weiss

12:30 - 1:00 P.M.
Reports and Conclusions

Reports from Work Groups
Conclusions & Summation

Child Care will be provided if requested in advance on Registration Form.

OUR FACULTY

* Viki DeJong is Chair of the Citizens Campaign for Civic Action. She is a leading environmental activist on Long Island. She is a retired teacher and a Past President of CRT.

* Marc A. Gruber is a rabbi serving Community Reform Temple, Westbury. He served for three years as National Co-Chair of New Jewish Agenda. He has spoken and published on a variety of issues of Jewish concern.

* Allan Mendels has 20 years experience in the insurance industry with a record of better than 90% policy retention for each year. He is in the top 2/10 of 1% of agents in the United States. He serves as a Director in the Roslyn Heights Civic Association.

* James E. Meyer is presently a sales and marketing Executive in private industry. For six years he served as Director of Alumni Relations and Development at Queens College.

* Ann Middleman is Principal of Ann Middleman Market Research and Consulting. With over 20 years in this business she has served in sales, marketing and public relations positions. For the past 3 years she has been writing publicity and press releases for C.R.T.

* Herb Oster taught in the NYC school system for ten years. He entered the life insurance business as a field representative for Guardian Life. After a short while he became a career development supervisor training new agents. He is a past president of CRT.

* Lydia Oster taught for four years in the NYC school system. She worked as an agent for Guardian Life Insurance Company. She became a supervisor for life and health insurance departments. Herb & Lydia now have their own financial services company.

* Larry Rothenberg currently serves the NY Federation of Reform Synagogues as a program Vice-President. He is Chair of the NY Fund for Reform Judaism. He served as President of Community Synagogue of Port Washington. He is an attorney practicing in a NYC firm.

* Robert Stein has sold radio advertising locally and nationally since 1963. He currently is a senior account executive at WALK FM/AM and has trained new salespeoples in the industry.

* Sue Weiss has 12 years experience as a social worker. Presently she is Social Work Supervisor at NCMC Child Development Center. Her duties include counseling, interviewing, and group work. She has served for two terms as CRT Recording Secretary.

* Robert Zimmerman is presently the Principal of Robert Zimmerman Public Relations. He has served as special consultant to the NY State Assembly Majority Leader.

RABBI'S MESSAGE
PASSOVER 1990

You are the future of Judaism. You guarantee not only that there will be a Jewish people, but also that there will be Judaism. There is a direct relationship between a person's synagogue affiliation and that individual's active of Jewish identification. People who affiliate with temples perpetuate Judaism in the most significant and rewarding ways.

We need to increase our congregation's membership, not simply to expand our financial base but, most importantly, to guarantee the vibrancy of our heritage and special way of life. Yes, the best way to stabilize your dues, and perhaps even reduce them, is to enlarge the number of households sharing the expenses. This will also enable Community Reform Temple to offer a wide range of programs, opportunities, and services to our members and our community.

I do not want to see our congregation become too large that we lose the **heimash** warmth which is so special here. Yet, there is room for growth. When we are a little larger and our financial well being is stronger, we will be able to offer even more creative programs and activities.

I have prepared a "Marketing & Membership Proposal" to the Board of Trustees. It includes strategies for recruiting new members and also for better involving members of our congregation. As part of our campaign I am making each of you a permanent member of the Membership Committee. We are having a workshop for all members of the Membership Committee (please read : **the entire Congregation**) on Sunday, May 6th. Please hold that morning free; circle it on your calendars NOW! Do not make any other plans on that day; cancel plans you have already made. This will be an opportunity for you to learn new skills, to express yourself, to learn about your own community, to give rise to latent talents, to have fun and to insure the well-being of our own congregation and Judaism.

If you would like a copy of my proposal, please see me or call the temple office and we will send you a copy.

I look forward to seeing you at the workshop.

Renee, Shai, Micah, and I wish each of you a joyous Pesach...

חג פסח ושמח

Marc Gruber

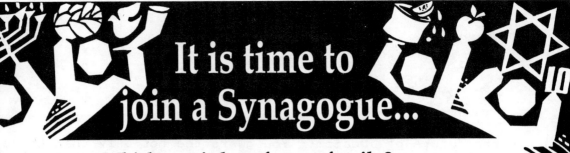

It is time to join a Synagogue...

Which one is best for my family?

What programs are available for all of us?

What will religious school do for my children?

The answers to these and all your questions will be answered by representatives from more than <u>fifteen</u> North Suburban Synagogues at the

North Suburban Synagogue Affiliation Day Fair

Sunday, August 11, 1991   10:00 A.M. - 1:00 P.M.
West Ridge Center • 636 Ridge Road • Highland Park, IL
(312) 782-1477

Congregations Participating

Beth Emet The Free Synagogue	Evanston, IL
B'nai Jehoshua Beth Elohim	Glenview, IL
Congregation Am Echod	Waukegan, IL
Congregation Beth Shalom	Northbrook, IL
Congregation Bnai Emunah	Skokie, IL
Congregation B'nai Tikvah	Deerfield, IL
Congregation Solel	Highland Park, IL
Jewish Reconstructionist Congregation	Evanston, IL
Lakeside Congregation for Reform Judaism	Highland Park, IL
Mikdosh El Hagro Hebrew Center	Evanston, IL
Moriah Congregation	Deerfield, IL
Niles Township Jewish Congregation	Skokie, IL
North Shore Congregation Israel	Glencoe, IL
North Suburban Synagogue Beth El	Highland Park, IL
Temple Beth Israel	Skokie, IL
Temple Jeremiah	Northfield, IL
Temple Judea Mizpah	Skokie, IL

Co-Sponsored by
The Union of American Hebrew Congregations
The United Synagogue of America
North Suburban Jewish Community Center

FREE	**FREE**	**FREE**
ADMISSION	**REFRESHMENTS**	**PARKING**

WILSHIRE BOULEVARD TEMPLE
B U L L E T I N

WEEK OF SEPTEMBER 3, 1990   PUBLISHED WEEKLY   VOLUME 77, NUMBER 36

Point of View…

Meet Me At The Fair

Fairs are fun. Attend a country fair and you get an instant insight into the folks and culture of the locale. You may even walk away with some delicious recipes or revelations for improving the quality of your life.

Fairs can open new worlds. I once met a man who grew the most beautiful begonias I ever saw in pots. Big green leaves topped with cascades of yellow, red, white and pink flowers. "How do you get them to grow so large?" I asked, embarrassed by the thought of my puny ones at home. He smiled. Sized me up, calculating if I was worthy of his secret. Leaning toward me, he whispered it in my ear. My begonias have never quite matched his, but they are prouder now each year.

So Wilshire Boulevard Temple is hosting a fair on Sunday morning, September 9, from 10:00 a.m. to 11:30 a.m. Why?

Because we have some secrets to share with you and your friends about our wonderful congregation and its myriad of activities.

We want you to invite your friends, members of your family, people you work with to join us. We will provide everything from coffee to bagels to inspiration. Those attending will have an opportunity to hear about our Religious School, and their children will be given a chance to sample a classroom experience. Tours of our exciting exhibit center and galleries, of our national landmark Sanctuary, of our day care/nursery school center, of our new chapel and children's library are arranged. Our rabbis will be there to answer questions about the philosophy of Wilshire Boulevard Temple. Leaders of the congregation will be present to talk about the activities of our camps, committees, Brotherhood, Sisterhood, Young Congregants, Seniors, Adult Education, "Where I Work" and "Where I Live"…and on and on from booth to booth. It's a fair!

And it will be fun. You bet it will. I have said this before in this place. I repeat it now. We need to encourage unaffiliated friends and family to join synagogues because, simply stated, the synagogue is the unique generator of our Jewish future.

So gather your friends and family and join us at the fair. Who knows, I may even share my secret for big beautiful begonias!

—Rabbi Harvey J. Fields

This isn't the only character Temple Beth El Hebrew School teaches.

In today's age, a Hebrew School teaches more than preparation for Bat and Bar Mitzvahs. It's the source of the essential life lessons that shape children into whom they'll always be. A Hebrew education touches on concepts like idealism, morality and dedication, words few of us hear frequently enough... and many of us yearn for. The Beth El Hebrew School understands this and teaches this, clearly. And even makes it seem like fun.

FREE KINDERGARTEN

As a means of making a good Jewish education attainable for even young families just starting out, the Beth El Board of Trustees has elected to eliminate tuition fees for every child in our kindergarten. We hope you will take advantage of this opportunity to provide a foundation for your child's future.
This Religious Outreach program is available only for those families that are not affiliated with any other congregation.

REGISTRATION
June 1, 12, 14
7:30 to 9:30 P.M.

SPECIAL REDUCED
MEMBERSHIP RATES
FOR YOUNG COUPLES.
CALL FOR DETAILS

Temple Beth El
415 Viola Road
Spring Valley, NY 10977
352-5823

Temple Emanu-El
of Lynbrook

One Saperstein Plaza
Lynbrook, New York 11563
(516) 593-4004

AN INVITATION TO JOIN TEMPLE EMANU-EL'S 1991-92
MEMBERHIP CAMPAIGN

July 22, 1991

Dear Fellow Temple Member:

As you well know, we are living in times where thoughts of finance and economics are uppermost in the minds of many of us. Temple Emanu-El must also deal with the need to find ways to increase financial support to meet ever increasing expenses.

This coming year we are embarking on a one-year experimental program to increase our membership. Aside from the added dollars, new members represent new ideas, new friendships, and new hands to implement our many volunteer-run activities.

In order to do this we want to use a mutual help approach: You Help Temple - Temple Helps You. Bring a new member into Temple and Temple will thank you by crediting your membership account by an amount equivalent to 25% of your annual dues (for a New Family Membership) or 12.5% (for a New Single Membership) for one year.

We all know lots of people: Perhaps you have:
    a) A New Neighbor;
    b) A Family in your child's school;
    c) A Friend at the office, club, gym, etc.

Tell them about Temple Emanu-El. Bring them to a Service or special program. As a Member, you already are familiar with the many activities and programs available at Temple Emanu-El such as Religious School, our High Holiday Services, our Lecture Series. You are our best representative when it comes to promoting our Temple.

We'll have informational packets ready for you which describe many of our activities to help you fill in the details. As of this time, dues credit will be limited to two new members per year.

If you are interested in joining the program, please fill out the enclosed response card. If you have any questions, please feel free to call me at 791-6689.

Sincerely Yours,

Ted Tsuruoka,
VP-Membership

Stuart M. Geller, Rabbi
Harold I. Saperstein, Rabbi Emeritus
Sue Hochberg, President

315 Barr Avenue, Woodmere, N.Y. 11598
170 Hempstead Avenue, Malverne, N.Y. 11565
176 Westview Lane, Hewlett, N.Y. 11557

569-4268
599-6794
374-5340

81

DOING JEWISH

Whether you were born Jewish
Are considering Judaism
Have chosen Judaism
Are raising Jewish children
Or just want to know more about Judaism:

Temple Emanu-El's

Doing Jewish
Workshops

can give you the answers

This series of **six free** monthly **workshops** is open to all. Join us and find out what you've been wanting to know, starting:

Tuesday, November 22, 1989
at 8 p.m.
Temple Emanu-El

EVERYONE IS WELCOME

To register, call **Temple Emanu-El at 549-4442**

This program presented by Temple Emanu-El Outreach

(Temple Emanu-El, Edison, NJ)

REACH OUT

The slogan "Reach Out and Touch Someone" has been publicized widely and has been very successful in motivating people to communicate with others, to share interests, and to cement friendships.

We would like to challenge the members of our congregation to "Reach Out and Touch Someone." Take the time to visit someone - to call someone on the telephone for a chat - to offer an invitation to someone to come along with you to attend services or one of the functions at our Temple. Reach out to newcomers to the community or to visitors to the Temple to make them feel the warmth of sincere hospitality. If you reach out to people, you will benefit from their gratitude and you will feel good about yourself.

Recently we had a wonderful opportunity to welcome a group of tourists from the Delta Queen tour, to visit with them in our Temple and to offer them our hospitality. Those of us who were there really enjoyed the visitors. In turn, they were very appreciative of our gracious "southern" hospitality.

Maurine W. Lipnick, President
Hebrew Union Congregation
Greenville, MS

Point of View...

Invite A Friend

We are into September. School is beginning for many of our children. Some of us have just returned from vacations, at least a mini-vacation over Labor Day Weekend. Most of us have that Jewish sixth-sense that the High Holy Days are approaching.

And we are right.

But first matters first.

It is time to introduce your friends, your families, your neighbors, those who might work with you—who are Jewish but unaffiliated with a synagogue—to the wonderful and vital world of Wilshire Boulevard Temple.

Some weeks ago, a friend told me that he had spoken with a neighbor about membership in a Temple as a part of our Wilshire Boulevard Temple outreach to the unaffiliated. "I just asked him if he had ever thought about joining a congregation. He nodded. So I pursued the matter. 'How come you've never joined Wilshire Boulevard Temple?' You'll never believe his response," my friend continued.

"What did he say?" I asked.

"He told me, 'No one ever invited me!'"

That is likely the reason why so many Jews remain unaffiliated. And we need to turn that situation around. A synagogue is the only institution in the Jewish world that *makes Jews* instead of *using Jews*. Those of us committed to the future of Jewish visions and values must begin *inviting* others to join us—to enjoy the benefits of belonging to a synagogue community.

So we have a special opportunity for you.

On Friday evening, September 15, at 8:15 p.m., we will celebrate a Late Shabbat evening service, which will include an opportunity for our members and those they invite to capture an insight into the varied programs offered, for all ages, at Wilshire Boulevard Temple. Our rabbis and lay leadership will be available for questions, for tours of our facilities, and to welcome, warmly, those who join us.

Here is a chance to "invite" friends, family and neighbors to visit your Temple, to show it off, and to share with them the benefits—and challenges—of belonging.

Plan to be with us on September 15.

—*Rabbi Harvey J. Fields*

(Wilshire Boulevard Temple, Los Angeles, CA)

DUES INFORMATION 1990-1991

The Dues and Membership policy of Shir Tikvah is very simple - If you want to be a member, you are a member. If you cannot afford what is listed below, we will help you. Once your dues are established, that becomes your "full" dues for the year. We would much rather have you as a member at reduced dues than not at all. We hope you feel the same.

Of course maintaining our congregation and the Jewish identity and presence in our area requires financial support from all members. Based on our budget needs, we have set the following dues schedule.

Our Couples membership dues are $640 a year. This category applies when the home contains two or more adults between age 30 and 65.

Our Singles membership dues are $400 a year and applies to singles between age 30 and 65.

Our third category, "Set-your-own-dues", is available to all those under 30 or over 65. If married, both husband and wife must satisfy the age requirement to qualify. This program recognizes that these groups usually have less income or need for our services. Because we are near capacity for the High Holidays, the minimum dues for this category is $90 per adult, the same rate we charge non-members for High Holiday tickets.

Under "Set-your-own-dues", you determine for yourself what you can afford and that becomes your dues. We do not require any applications or interviews. Since most of the income we need to pay expenses comes from dues, we do ask all in this category to give what they can afford.

Since these three categories cannot anticipate all circumstances, our Executive Committee accepts confidential requests for dues reduction based on need. You can discuss this in whatever manner you are most comfortable - by calling or writing a member of the Executive Committee or by talking with a Co-Chair of the Membership Committee who will then speak for you at an Executive Committee meeting. We do not require any records to support such a request. Our policy is to never deny membership because of financial limitations.

We have no building fund. We do own land in Troy at the corner of Wattles and Northfield Parkway which is intended for eventual use as a Temple. We do not expect to begin this project until we are large enough so that the obligation is affordable to all.

Our dues year is from April 1 to March 31. Dues may be paid in 1, 2, or 4 installments. Bills are sent 1 month before the due date. Full dues regardless of category apply to members joining between April 1 and the High Holidays with a 50% reduction if joining between the Holidays and Dec. 31 and pro-rated thereafter.

Our Hebrew and Religious schools are staffed by the United Hebrew Schools. Information and tuition are available upon request.

To join, call our Treasurer, Barry Gerall (377-8054). Thank you for considering Shir Tikvah. We invite you to belong and share.

(Congregation Shir Tikvah, Troy, MI)

SECTION B. INTEGRATION

This section contains suggestions
and programmatic ideas to help
congregations design ways to
welcome and involve their new
members. A model curriculum for
a "New Member Class" is included,
along with supplementary
materials from congregations.

INTEGRATION OF NEW MEMBERS

A family who recently joined a synagogue walks in for Rosh Hashanah services. They just moved to the community ... they don't know anyone, not even the rabbi ... they have never been to a Reform service before.

Congregations have a window of opportunity in the first few months after new members join to welcome them into the community, orient them, excite them about being part of the congregation and motivate them to become involved. New members need an active program of integration in order to feel that they can become part of the community. Barriers to successful integration can cause membership to be unsatisfactory and shallow, potentially leading to low-intensity involvement or premature resignation from the congregation. The future of a congregation depends on its ability to grasp that moment when new members join; fully integrating new members into temple life will energize the congregation and be the first step in developing committed members whose lives will be enhanced by their temple connection and who will in turn contribute to the life of the congregation.

I. Needs of New Members

What is it that new members need when they join a temple? To a certain extent, their needs will vary depending upon the size of your congregation:

A. *Small Congregations (A,AB)*

New members need ...

1. to learn about the heritage and the traditions of the congregation.

2. to gain acceptance and recognition by members *outside* of temple functions.

3. to become acquainted with key congregants, the official and unofficial "heads of the family".

4. to find a safe environment in which to discuss this new relationship with the synagogue "family".

B. *Medium Congregations (B,C)*

New members need ...

1. attention and caring during the initial stages of entry into the congregation.

2. various planned opportunities to become involved in the temple and to establish contacts;

3. introductions to 8-10 members, several of whom should share common interests

C. *Large congregations (C-E)*

New members need ...

1. a "road map" to the life and functions of the congregation.

2. a process of specific steps to follow in order to find their place and become involved in the congregation

3. recognition and respect as a person, not just another new member

II. Welcoming New Members

A. In their homes

* Welcome Wagon - have members deliver a welcome basket to all new members which might include

  — a bottle of wine
  — Shabbat candles
  — a challah (or certificate redeemable for a challah)
  — a "Do-It-Yourself Shabbat" brochure (available from UAHC Press)
  — "Come Let Us Welcome Shabbat" (a cassette and tape booklet of Shabbat prayers and songs available through the UAHC Department of Education)
  — *Gates of Shabbat* (a booklet with prayers and songs for Shabbat available through the CCAR)
  — a packet of materials from the temple describing temple services, programs and committees

B. In the temple

* Buddy System - many congregations set up a buddy system, pairing long-term members with new members. Buddies contact the new members and welcome them to the temple, offer to help them (i.e., getting in a car pool), invite them to join them for services and other programs. Buddies should also contact the new member at different points throughout the member's first year to see how things are going. In many cases, it works out better not to have a one-to-one matching, but to assign two long-term couples to one new couple, for example. Give buddies a brief letter outlining their responsibilities and providing the name of a person to call with questions. Choose buddies who are familiar with the temple and its programs.

  — Temple Rodeph Torah of Western Monmouth (Marlboro, NJ) involves the past year's new members to serve as buddies for the present year's new members. At the end of the year, the rabbi contacts the committee members, thanks them for their services and asks them to join different committees. Then the present year's new members become the committee for next year's new members.

  — Monmouth Reform Temple (Tinton Falls, NJ) established CONTACT - "Creating Opportunities for Newcomers Through Active Congregational Ties". The Membership Chair invites active congregants to participate in this program by serving as contact people for newcomers. Contact people invite the new members to temple activities and offer to take them or meet them there. During the year postcards are sent to the contact people with upcoming temple events and a reminder to contact the new members. The CONTACT program enables newcomers to feel more comfortable in the temple.

* Temple Bulletin - list the names and addresses of new members with special words of welcome

* New Member Shabbat - designate a special Shabbat to welcome new members.

  — Ask new members to participate in different parts of the service.
  — Address issues of membership in the sermon.
  — Ask new members to recite a special prayer.
  — Present new members with a gift: *Gates of the House, Gates of Prayer, Gates of Shabbat,* or *Gates of Repentance* (CCAR), or *The Jewish Home,* by Rabbi Daniel Syme (UAHC Press).
  — Have a New Members' Shabbat dinner preceeding services and invite

some of last year's new members and representatives of the lay and professional leadership.

*   Place photos of new members in the temple lobby with a special welcome sign.

III. Integrating New Members into the Congregation

A. Membership intake form - all new members should fill out a form which asks for basic demographic information, religious background, former temple membership, etc. as well as skills, areas of interests, and activities/committees that they would like to be involved in. (See samples that follow)

    *   Develop a SKILLS BANK to keep track of the skills of all members so that you can call upon them when needed

    *   Pass on the names of new members to the appropriate committees for the areas in which they indicated interest. BE SURE COMMITTEE CHAIRS FOLLOW THROUGH IN CONTACTING THE NEW MEMBERS — BY ASKING FOR THE INFORMATION YOU CREATE THE EXPECTATION THAT SOMEONE WILL CONTACT THEM. DON'T DISAPPOINT THEM.

B. Responses for Different Size Congregations

    1. Especially for the *Small* Congregation:

    *   arrange a visit with a senior member, someone who was a key leader in the life of the temple or who is familiar with the history of the congregation, who can recount the heritage and traditions of the congregation.

    *   provide a brief written history of the temple and a membership roster.

    *   ask family and/or friends of the newcomers, who are temple members, to serve as guides into synagogue life.

    *   take interest in and learn about the new members; seek out opportunities for them to interact with temple leadership.

    *   ask members to build a warm relationship with newcomers, both inside and outside of temple

    *   clergy can serve as "confidant" for newcomers and offer them his/her services

    2. Especially for the *Medium* Congregation:

    *   identify members who can be hosts and hostesses; they must be people who are active in the congregation and know those in the leadership circle

    *   make one or two people "chairs of hospitality" (announce it in a public way — at a service, in the bulletin) whose task is to learn about new members and oversee their integration into the congregation in their first six months of membership. Suggested activities:
        1. match new members with suitable members and groups
        2. make appropriate introductions at congregational gatherings
        3. provide the newcomers with necessary orientation
        4. host events where newcomers will have contact with clergy
        5. let clergy know when new members want visits from them

    *   emphasize in the congregation that it is the responsibility of *all* members to

welcome and greet the newcomers, to create an inviting atmosphere (it is best *not* to form a separate "new member" committee).

* create opportunities for orientation and education for new members, such as a "New Member Class" (see model curriculum in this section)

3. Especially for the *Large* Congregation:

* Create an incorporation program which includes

    1. providing a warm welcome
        — train greeters for worship services
        — train entire membership to be welcoming

    2. providing opportunities for orientation and education (Basic Judaism, New Member Classes)

    3. finding a place to belong
        — orientation about options for new members before they attend committee meetings
        — appoint "hosts" to guide them along
        — introduce them to groups of members with similar interests

    4. monitoring progress and satisfaction during *first year*
        — appoint individuals who will watch for disappointments among new members (good positions for senior members)

    5. membership care teams
        — help new members, meet with lapsed members
        — need training and supervision by clergy

    6. administration
        — assign staff member to coordinate a program of attracting and assimilating new members

C. Practical Suggestions

* offer New Member Classes to introduce new members to your temple and to Reform Judaism (see model curriculum in this section)

* require an orientation session for parents of children entering religious school

* Monmouth Reform Temple (Tinton Falls, NJ) has created a program called "Mitzvot of Membership", that addresses the commitment expected of members in the areas of study, worship and community. New members are encouraged to make a spiritual pledge during the High Holy Days. (See text in the pages that follow)

* New member Orientation Evenings - invite new members to a dinner (or just have dessert) in their honor at which they can meet other new members and long-standing members. Arrange for hosts to pick people up and sit with them through the evening. The lay leadership can share with new members the various ways in which they can get involved in temple life. (If they can make up a skit or do it in a fun way, it will also provide some entertainment.) The clergy and professional staff should also be part of the evening.

* In addition to holding several new member coffees at which new members can learn about temple activities, Temple Shalom (Succasunna, NJ) also

sponsors social activities especially for new members.

* Jewish Community Center (White Plains, NY) has a New Members Network, composed of all members who join during a particular year. The goal is to provide a comfortable way for those who want to get involved to meet other new members. A steering committee calls each new member and invites them to services, special Temple programs and new members events. At the end of the year the group disperses and a new group is formed.

* appoint one person from the "New Member Class" or new member group to represent new members to the Board of Trustees.

* Solel Congregation (Mississauga, Ontario, CANADA) holds quarterly Community Shabbat Dinners that are open to the unaffiliated as well as to members. Members take turns preparing the food; one group will teach another how to prepare traditional Shabbat meals. A Shabbat booklet containing the blessings and songs is provided for participants to take home. Informal teaching about Shabbat takes place throughout the evening.

NEW MEMBER CLASS

Upon joining a congregation, new members have a variety of basic needs that must be met in order for them to feel part of the community. They need to be welcomed in a special way, introduced to the lay and professional leadership, given an in-depth guided tour of the temple and led through processes such as religious school registration. Having learned the answers to the basic questions "who, what, where, when and how", new members can find their way around the congregation and, at least from the outside, appear as if they are part of the community. But, as of yet, they have not learned the answer to the most important question: "why". Why be a temple member? Why be a member of this congregation? What does belonging to this congregation mean to me? What expectations do I have of my membership? What does the temple expect of me?

One way to help new members explore the "whys" of temple membership is by offering a *New Members Class* to each incoming group of new members. Every congregation has its legends and myths, its sacred events and sense of self. To the extent that, through a *New Members Class,* we can successfully transmit that communal identity to new members and make them feel that they belong, the more successful will be their involvement. The following are suggested guidelines and an outline of a model curriculum for organizing such a class.

GOALS

1. to enable new members to understand the meaning of temple membership and develop a personal connection to their temple

2. to enhance integration into the life of the congregation through learning about its history, religious practices and distinctive character.

3. to increase familiarity with the temple itself

4. to build bonds between new members and provide a community for them within the congregation

5. to develop a personal connection between the rabbi and new members

6. to encourage new members' active participation in temple life

LOGISTICS:

1. Conduct the class in four to six weekly sessions, meeting for an hour and a half to two hours at each session.

2. Begin early in the Fall, immediately following Simchat Torah.

3. The rabbi (or rabbis) should extend the invitation to new members to participate in the class and should personally lead the class. A personal connection with the rabbi is vital for feeling valued and for forming long-term connections with the congregation.

4. If you have a Cantor, invite him/her to teach some of the songs and prayers in Session 3.

5. Invite a lay leader to the last session to share his/her personal story of involvement in temple life and what temple membership means to them. Try to select a person who can speak well before a group in an informal and open manner.

6. Allow the class to be a dialogue between the rabbi and new members, not a lecture class.

7. Throughout the class, give participants the opportunity to learn about the backgrounds of other congregants (that they also come from a variety of backgrounds, maybe not Reform, maybe interfaith, etc.) and to share ideas and visions. These connections are one of the most important reasons that people join congregations.

8. Encourage participants to attend temple activities by going together. Organize a New Member Class Shabbat dinner prior to attendance at Shabbat services, for example. By attending as a group, they can make an unfamiliar situation more comfortable and inviting.

GETTING STARTED:

1. It is very important for the success of the class that participation in it be stressed as a given when potential members express an interest in membership. While participation in a New Members Class cannot be made a "requirement" of membership per se, it can become an expectation of temple life.

2. Members of the membership committee, the temple administrator and anyone who meets with potential members should encourage attendance at the New Member Class.

3. Send a personal invitation from the rabbi to all new members who have joined since the last class was offered, inviting them to participate in the class.

4. Make follow-up phone calls as well.

5. Many new members may be families with young children, so offering child care will help increase attendance.

6. Give participants materials to help in their integration into the congregation, such as:
    *   brochures about the temple,
    *   recent temple bulletins,
    *   transliteration sheets for Shabbat services,
    *   samples of publicity from programs,
    *   temple constitution,
    *   a guide to understanding the temple structure,
    *   a membership directory
    *   copy of *Reform Judaism*

    It would also be nice to present participants with a book about Judaism or Reform Judaism, or at least a suggested reading list which might include:
    *   *Gates of Shabbat*, (CCAR),
    *   *The Jewish Home*, Rabbi Daniel B. Syme (UAHC Press),
    *   *Everyperson's Guide to Judaism*, Lydia Kukoff (UAHC Press)
    *   *Liberal Judaism at Home*, Morrison David Bial (UAHC)

7. Hand out an evaluation form at the last class to obtain feedback from participants and learn how you can improve the class for next year. (See sample form following model curriculum.)

NEW MEMBERS CLASS

CURRICULUM

The following is a five session model which can easily be adapted to each congregation's needs. This curriculum is derived from the examples of congregations that have offered successful programs (in particular, Anshe Emeth Memorial Temple in New Brunswick, NJ and Temple Beth David in Westminster, CA). A teacher's guide expanding upon the outline presented here is in development.

Session 1:   Welcome to (Temple Name)

Introduction of rabbi and class members.

A guided discussion of why people joined, their personal religious backgrounds, what they hope to gain from membership in a Reform congregation, what questions they have.

Discussion of the historical and contemporary role of the synagogue in Jewish life. The importance of membership.

Session 2:   Reform Judaism

The history, development and ideology of the Reform movement, what we believe and what we do.

The ABC's of the Reform movement.

Dimensions of Jewish spirituality. Discussion of personal spirituality.

Session 3:   Our Synagogue

History, legends, myths and mission of this congregation — its characters, leaders and traditions.

An introduction to the liturgical practices in our congregation, especially the music.

Session 4:   Ritual and Practice

Holiday and life cycle practices in our congregation. Why we do what we do.

Coordination between home and synagogue celebrations.

Session 5:   The Challenge of Synagogue Involvement - My Role

The covenant of membership (See "Mitzvot of Membership" in this section, as an example).

"Why I am an active temple member" - shared personal experience of lay leader.

Opportunities for involvement in synagogue life, including an overview of programs.

New Members Class
Evaluation Form

1. The class met four sessions. Was that
___too many   ___too few   ___the right number.
If too many or too few, how many sessions should the class last?__

2. Please rate the value of each session on a scale of 1 to 5; if a session was very worthwhile, rate it 1 and if not worthwhile at all, rate it 5, or somewhere in between.

		1	2	3	4	5

Week 1, History of synagogues
Week 2, Reform Judaism
Week 3, Liturgy and Life Cycle
Week 4, History and characters
        of Beth David
For any sessions you rated 3, 4, or 5, please describe why it was not worthwhile and what you would change (including the possibility of eliminating that topic):

3. Are there topics we did not include that we should have? Which ones?

4. Not all new members participated in the program. What barriers do you think played a role in deciding whether to participate:
___Childcare
___Interest in the program
___Schedule conflicts

5. Should this program be offered for each "class" of new members?

6. What changes in the program would you propose?

7. How do you think this class will affect your integration into and involvement in the congregation?

8. What should the rabbi and/or the lay leaders of Temple Beth David be doing differently to welcome new members of the congregation?

Additional helpful comments:

MITZVOT OF MEMBERSHIP

By Rabbi Sally Priesand
Monmouth Reform Temple
Tinton Falls, New Jersey

Every synagogue has the responsibility of providing for its members a well-rounded, diverse program of activities which touches every area of Jewish life. We know that to be true; indeed, we take it for granted, but we sometimes forget that synagogue membership is a two-way street. If the synagogue is obligated to provide certain activities, then surely its members are obligated to participate in them. Joining a congregation is like entering into a covenant; both parties have responsibilities, and the synagogue cannot really function at its best unless those obligations are met.

Worship, education, community - these are the goals of every synagogue. As you become part of our Temple family, we are grateful for your financial support, but we hope you will want to contribute toward the survival of Judaism and the Jewish people in other ways as well. Indeed, we ask you to become partners with us in creating an institution that will truly be a storehouse of the Jewish spirit. We want our synagogue to be a place where we can give thanks to God, explore the richness of our heritage, and be reminded that we are part of a people whose mission it is to perfect the world. We want our synagogue to be an extended family in which people are willing to be there for each other, a place where we can find comfort in time of trouble, courage and hope when in doubt or difficulty, and when in joy, a celebration of our happiness. We want our synagogue to be a place where we can create memories for our children, memories so powerful that they will seek to pass them on to their children and their children's children. We want our synagogue to be a place which encourages its members to take responsibility for their own Jewishness.

It is in this spirit, then, that we present to you the following Mitzvot of Membership. We hope you will use this list as a guide in determining your own level of involvement and participation in Temple activities. Please know that the more you are able to do, the greater the possibilities for personal enrichment and the more you will feel part of our Temple family.

Beit Tefillah - House of Prayer

Attend worship services regularly.

Participate on the bima when asked.

Think about the role of spirituality in your life.

Observe Shabbat.

Celebrate Holydays and festivals.

Follow Jewish customs and ceremonies.

Translate words of prayer into deeds of justice and thereby make a difference in our community and our world.

Beit Midrash - House of Study

Make study of Torah a regular part of your life.

Participate in Adult Education programs.

Share in your child's religious education and re-inforce it at home.

Use our Temple library.

Discuss Jewish values with your family and be aware of the ways in which they are reflected in your daily life.

Help to make our synagogue a caring community by reaching out to others.

Visit the sick.

Comfort the mourner.

Welcome the stranger.

Call those whom you haven't seen at Temple lately and let them know they've been missed.

Host the Oneg Shabbat when asked.

Support the work of Temple auxiliaries.

Join a committee.

Attend the Annual Meeting.

Volunteer your time for special projects.

Be knowledgeable about Temple by reading the bulletin and other communications.

Respond to questionnaires and other requests for information so that your views can be taken into consideration when decisions are made about synagogue priorities.

Make every effort to attend special programs.

Support the work of the larger Jewish community.

Be an ambassador for the State of Israel and oppressed Jews throughout the world.

Contribute tzedakah to Temple funds and charities of your own choosing on a regular basis.

north shore congregation israel

1185 Sheridan Road • Glencoe, Illinois 60022
312/835-0724

MEMBERSHIP FAMILY RECORD
(Please print or type)

Date Prepared_____

	Adult Male	Adult Female
1. Full Name: Last, First & Middle Int.		
Prefer to be called		
2. Title you prefer:	Dr. ☐ Mr. ☐ Other ☐	Dr. ☐ Mrs. ☐ Ms. ☐ Other ☐
3. Address, City State & Zip		
4. Home Phone:		
Second Address: From_____To_____		
5. Current marital status	☐ Married ☐ Single ☐ Divorced ☐ Widowed	☐ Married ☐ Single ☐ Divorced ☐ Widowed
If married, Date of marriage	Month:_____ Day:_____Year:_____	Month:_____Day:_____Year:_____
7. Place of birth:	City:_____State:_____Country:_____	City: _____ State: _____ Country: _____
8. Date of birth:	Month: _____ Day: _____ Year: _____	Month:_____Day:_____Year:_____
9. Parents' names: (Please enter full names)	Father: _____ ☐ Living ☐ Deceased Date of death_____ Mother: _____ ☐ Living ☐ Deceased Date of death_____ ☐ Members of North Shore Congregation Israel?	Father: _____ ☐ Living ☐ Deceased Date of death_____ Mother: _____ ☐ Living ☐ Deceased Date of death_____ ☐ Members of North Dhore Congregation Israel?
10. Occupation	Job Description: _____ ☐ Full Time ☐ Part Time ☐ Retired ☐ Unemployed Title: _____ Employer: _____ Business Address_____ Business Phone_____Ext._____	Job Description: _____ ☐ Full Time ☐ Part Time ☐ Retired ☐ Unemployed Title: _____ Employer: _____ Business Address_____ Business Phone_____Ext._____
11. Education: (Please check highest education level and name of degree)	☐ High School ☐ College ☐ Degree ☐ Graduate School ☐ Degree Other:_____	☐ High School ☐ College ☐ Degree ☐ Graduate School ☐ Degree Other:_____

12. Religious tradition in which you were raised (Check One) If not raised in the Jewish tradition are you (Check one) Did your Jewish education Include: (Check appropriate boxes)	☐ Reform ☐ Conservative ☐ Orthodox ☐ Secular ☐ Jewish by Choice ☐ Non-Jewish Denomination: _____ ☐ Bar Mitzvah Date_____Confirmation Date_____ Congregation Name:_____ City _____ State _____	☐ Reform ☐ Conservative ☐ Orthodox ☐ Secular ☐ Jewish by choice ☐ Non-Jewish Denomination: _____ ☐ Bat Mitzvah Date_____Confirmation Date_____ Congregation Name:_____ City:_____State:_____
13. Do you own cemetery property? (Check appropriate boxes)	☐ Yes ☐ No If so, is the property at:(Please check one) ☐ Shalom Memorial Park ☐ Other_____	☐ Yes ☐ No If so, is the property at:(Please check one) ☐ Shalom Memorial Park ☐ Other:_____
14. Do you read Hebrew?	☐ Yes ☐ No	☐ Yes ☐ No
15. Do you wish to participate in services?	☐ Yes ☐ No ☐ English portion ☐ Hebrew portion	☐ Yes ☐ No ☐ English portion ☐ Hebrew portion
16. ·· case of emergency the Temple is to notify: (Include name, address & phone number)		
17. Date joined North Shore Congregation Israel:		

PLEASE FILL IN THE FOLLOWING INFORMATION AS IT APPLIES TO EACH OF YOUR CHILDREN

1. Name (Also nickname)					
2. Address (If different from yours, including City, State, Zip)					
3. Date of Birth					
4. Sex	☐ Male ☐ Female	☐ Male ☐ Female	☐ Male ☐ Female	☐ Male ☐ Female	☐ Male ☐ Female
Marital Status Spouse's Name					
6. Religious School	☐ Attended ☐ Attending Grade_____	☐ Attended ☐ Attending Grade_____	☐ Attended ☐ Attending Grade_____	☐ Attended ☐ Attending Grade_____	☐ Attended ☐ Attending Grade_____
7. Hebrew School	☐ Attended ☐ Attending Grade_____	☐ Attended ☐ Attending Grade_____	☐ Attended ☐ Attending Grade_____	☐ Attended ☐ Attending Grade_____	☐ Attended ☐ Attending Grade_____
8. Bar/Bat Mitzvah	☐ Yes ☐ No Date _____	☐ Yes ☐ No Date _____	☐ Yes ☐ No Date _____	☐ Yes ☐ No Date _____	☐ Yes ☐ No Date _____
9. Confirmation	☐ Yes ☐ No Date _____	☐ Yes ☐ No Date _____	☐ Yes ☐ No Date _____	☐ Yes ☐ No Date _____	☐ Yes ☐ No Date _____
10. Currently in Temple Youth Group	☐ Yes ☐ No	☐ Yes ☐ No	☐ Yes ☐ No	☐ Yes ☐ No	☐ Yes ☐ No

CONGREGATION ACTIVITIES IN WHICH YOU ARE INTERESTED AND WOULD LIKE TO PARTICIPATE

INDICATE INTERESTS BY CHECK MARKS	ADULT MALE	ADULT FEMALE	INDICATE INTERESTS BY CHECK MARKS	ADULT MALE	ADULT FEMALE
Adult Education			Religious School		
Archives			Worship Committee		
Art & Beautification			Retirement Group		
Brotherhood			Room Mother		
Budget			Senior Group		
Building & Grounds			Single Parents		
Caring Committee/Visitation of Sick			Singles		
Cemetery			Sisterhood		
Chavurah			Social Action		
Choir Group			Temple Board		
Communication (Bulletin)			Temple Guide		
Cooking			Transportation		
Fine Arts & Displays			Usher Corps		
Fund Raising			High Holidays		
Judaica Shop Volunteer			Sabbath Services		
High Holiday			Young Marrieds (Couples Club)		
Israel			Youth Group		
Library			Host at Sabbath Kiddush Table		
Membership			Reader at Sabbath Service		
Music			[ ] English [ ] Hebrew		
Nominating			Other		
Public Relations					
			Have someone call me at		

SPECIAL SKILLS, TALENTS AND HOBBIES

INDICATE INTERESTS BY CHECK MARKS	ADULT MALE	ADULT FEMALE	INDICATE INTERESTS BY CHECK MARKS	ADULT MALE	ADULT FEMALE
Accounting			Hospitality		
Archives			Legal		
Art-Museum			Medical		
Clerical-Office Volunteer			Musical Instruments (List)		
Cooking			Reading from Torah		
Counseling			Teaching		
Crafts			Other (List)		
Financial					
Add any of N.S.C.I. needs			Other languages spoken		

Do you know anyone whom we should contact to join North Shore Congregation Israel?

Name _____ Phone _____

Address _____ Village _____

	ADULT MALE	ADULT FEMALE
Do you have any physical limitations of of which we should be aware?	☐ Vision ☐ Hearing ☐ Mobility Other (Specify) _____	☐ Vision [ ] Hearing [ ] Mobility Other (Specify) _____

TEMPLE EMANUEL
MAY AND CHANDLER STREETS, WORCESTER, MASS. 01602
TELEPHONE: 755-1257

MEMBERSHIP

APPLICATION

NAME _____

STREET _____

CITY _____ STATE _____ ZIP _____

PHONE _____

DATE _____

MARITAL STATUS
Single ☐   Married ☐   Divorced ☐   Separated ☐
Widowed ☐ If married, Date of Marriage ___/___/___ Mo. Day Year

	ADULT MALE	ADULT FEMALE
Full Name		Maiden Name (If not used):
Date of Birth		
Occupation and/or Position (Former if Retired)		
Name of Business	Retired ☐	Retired ☐
Business Phone		
Business Address		
Education	High School _____ College _____ Graduate School _____ Other _____	High School _____ College _____ Graduate School _____ Other _____
College(s) Attended (if any)		
Major Field		
Religious tradition in which you were raised	☐ Reform ☐ Secular, Non-Practicing ☐ Conservative ☐ Non-Jewish ☐ Orthodox ☐ None	☐ Reform ☐ Secular, Non-Practicing ☐ Conservative ☐ Non-Jewish ☐ Orthodox ☐ None
If not raised in the Jewish tradition, are you:	☐ Jewish by Choice ☐ Other	☐ Jewish by Choice ☐ Other
Do you wish to participate in services?	☐ Yes ☐ No ☐ Aliyot ☐ Read Torah ☐ Candle Lighting	☐ Yes ☐ No ☐ Aliyot ☐ Read Torah ☐ Candle Lighting
Do you have any disabilities?	☐ Hearing ☐ Walking ☐ None ☐ Vision ☐ Other	☐ Hearing ☐ Walking ☐ None ☐ Vision ☐ Other

101

Religious Education Experience	Adult Male	Adult Female
Religious School	☐ Attended ☐ Did not Attend	☐ Attended ☐ Did not Attend
Hebrew School	☐ Attended ☐ Did not Attend	☐ Attended ☐ Did not Attend
Jewish Day School	☐ Attended ☐ Did not Attend	☐ Attended ☐ Did not Attend
Bar/Bat Mitzvah	☐ Yes ☐ No	☐ Yes ☐ No
Confirmation	☐ Yes ☐ No	☐ Yes ☐ No
Post Confirmation Class	☐ Attended ☐ Did not Attend	☐ Attended ☐ Did not Attend
Jewish Camp	☐ Yes ☐ No	☐ Yes ☐ No
Temple/ Synagogue Youth Group	☐ Yes ☐ No	☐ Yes ☐ No
Adult Bar/Bat Mitzvah	☐ Yes ☐ No	☐ Yes ☐ No
Vistit to Israel	☐ Yes ☐ No	☐ Yes ☐ No

PLEASE CHECK (√) JEWISH ORGANIZATIONS YOU ARE AFFILIATED WITH AND THOSE IN WHICH YOU HAVE HELD OFFICE OR SERVED ON COMMITTEES.

ORGANIZATION	ADULT MALE Affiliated	ADULT MALE Office/Committee	ADULT FEMALE Affiliated	ADULT FEMALE Office/Committee
Anti-Defamation League	☐	☐	☐	☐
ARZA	☐	☐	☐	☐
B'nai B'rith	☐	☐	☐	☐
Brandeis	☐	☐	☐	☐
Dysautonomia Foundation	☐	☐	☐	☐
Federation	☐	☐	☐	☐
Hadassah	☐	☐	☐	☐
Jewish Community Center	☐	☐	☐	☐
Jewish Family Service	☐	☐	☐	☐
Jewish Home for the Aged	☐	☐	☐	☐
Jewish National Fund	☐	☐	☐	☐
Jewish War Veterans	☐	☐	☐	☐
Jewish Service Center for Older Adults	☐	☐	☐	☐
National Council of Jewish Women	☐	☐	☐	☐
ORT	☐	☐	☐	☐
ZOA	☐	☐	☐	☐
Other	☐	☐	☐	☐

TALENTS, ABILITIES & SKILLS — PLEASE CHECK (√)

	Male	Female		Male	Female
Art			Sewing		
Athletics			Singing		
Camping and Scouting			Woodwork		
Clerical			Other		
Cooking			LANGUAGE SKILLS:		
Crafts			Hebrew		
Creative Writing			Yiddish		
Dancing			Russian		
Drama			German		
Journalism			French		
Library			Italian		
Musical Instrument			Spanish		
Painting			Ladino		
Photography					

TEMPLE EMANUEL INVOLVEMENT CHECK (√) ALL THAT APPLY TO YOU, PAST AND PRESENT

MALE

☐ Temple Officer
☐ Temple Committees
☐ Temple Board
☐ Activities & Friendly Relations
☐ Adult Education
☐ Brotherhood
☐ Chavurah
☐ Finance
☐ Fine Arts
☐ High Holiday Usher
☐ Library
☐ Long Range Planning
☐ Membership

☐ Memorials & Capital Funds
☐ Music
☐ Nominating
☐ Outreach
☐ Personnel & Evaluation
☐ Properties
☐ Public Relations & Publicity
☐ School Committee
☐ Singles
☐ Social Action/Israel
☐ Worship
☐ Young Marrieds
☐ Youth

FEMALE

☐ Temple Officer
☐ Temple Committees
☐ Temple Board
☐ Activities & Friendly Relations
☐ Adult Education
☐ Chavurah
☐ Finance
☐ Fine Arts
☐ High Holiday Usher
☐ Library
☐ Long Range Planning
☐ Membership
☐ Memorials & Capital Funds

☐ Music
☐ Nominating
☐ Outreach
☐ Personnel & Evaluation
☐ Properties
☐ Public Relations & Publicity
☐ School Committee
☐ Singles
☐ Sisterhood
☐ Social Action/Israel
☐ Worship
☐ Young Marrieds
☐ Youth

When did you personally join Temple Emanuel? _____

Do you currently belong to another congregation in Worcester?

    ☐ Yes ☐ No If Yes, which one? _____

    Have you ever belonged to another congregation in Worcester?

    ☐ Yes ☐ No If Yes, which one?

In order to assist the congregation in scheduling activities, please complete the following questions:

    Do you spend a significant part of the year away from Worcester? ☐ Yes ☐ No

    If Yes, what months? _____

    How often does your family spend the week end out of town? _____

    Do you plan to move out of the Worcester area in the next 5 years? ☐ Yes ☐ No

YARZHEIT RECORD: (English Calendar _____ or Hebrew Calendar _____)

Name: _____ Relationship: _____ Date: _____

Name: _____ Relationship: _____ Date: _____

Name: _____ Relationship: _____ Date: _____

Name: _____ Relationship: _____ Date: _____

Name: _____ Relationship: _____ Date: _____

Name: _____ Relationship: _____ Date: _____

Name: _____ Relationship: _____ Date: _____

Name: _____ Relationship: _____ Date: _____

PLEASE FILL IN THE FOLLOWING INFORMATION AS IT APPLIES TO EACH OF YOUR CHILDREN UNDER AGE 25:

Name:					
Date of Birth:					
Sex:	☐ Male ☐ Female	☐ Male ☐ Female	☐ Male ☐ Female	☐ Male ☐ Female	☐ Male ☐ Female
Religious School:	☐ Attended ☐ Attending ☐ Will Attend	☐ Attended ☐ Attending ☐ Will Attend	☐ Attended ☐ Attending ☐ Will Attend	☐ Attended ☐ Attending ☐ Will Attend	☐ Attended ☐ Attending ☐ Will Attend
Jewish Day School	☐ Attended ☐ Attending ☐ Will Attend	☐ Attended ☐ Attending ☐ Will Attend	☐ Attended ☐ Attending ☐ Will Attend	☐ Attended ☐ Attending ☐ Will Attend	☐ Attended ☐ Attending ☐ Will Attend
Bar/Bat Mitzvah	☐ Yes ☐ No	☐ Yes ☐ No	☐ Yes ☐ No	☐ Yes ☐ No	☐ Yes ☐ No
Confirmation	☐ Yes ☐ No	☐ Yes ☐ No	☐ Yes ☐ No	☐ Yes ☐ No	☐ Yes ☐ No
Visit to Israel	☐ Yes ☐ No	☐ Yes ☐ No	☐ Yes ☐ No	☐ Yes ☐ No	☐ Yes ☐ No
Jewish Camp Experience	☐ Yes ☐ No	☐ Yes ☐ No	☐ Yes ☐ No	☐ Yes ☐ No	☐ Yes ☐ No
Temple Youth Group	☐ Yes ☐ No	☐ Yes ☐ No	☐ Yes ☐ No	☐ Yes ☐ No	☐ Yes ☐ No

From your own experience, what do you consider the greatest strengths of Temple Emanuel?

From your experience, what areas of Temple Emanuel need improvement?

104

TEMPLE JEREMIAH

937 Happ Road - P.O. Box 8209
Northfield, Illinois 60093
441-5760

APPLICATION FOR MEMBERSHIP

Date _____ 19 _____

We (I) hereby apply for membership in Temple Jeremiah, a congregation dedicated to the principles of Reform Judaism. Our primary goals are the enhancement of our religious experience, the continuing education of our members and their children, and a commitment to humanity.

FAMILY RECORD

MAILING NAME AND ADDRESS

Name _____

Number & Street _____

City & State _____ Zip Code _____

Telephone Number _____

MARITAL STATUS

☐ Married (Date of Marriage) _____/_____/_____

☐ Single (never married), ☐ Separated

☐ Widowed ☐ Divorced

MALE

First & Middle Names _____

Hebrew Name (If applicable) _____

Date of Birth _____/_____/_____

Occupation _____

Business Name _____

Business Address _____

Business City & State _____ Zip Code _____

Business Telephone _____

RELIGIOUS BACKGROUND

☐ Reform ☐ Conservative ☐ Orthodox ☐ None

☐ Non Jewish (Religion Practiced) _____

☐ Convert to Judaism (year) _____

Date of Bar Mitzvah _____/_____/_____ Year of Confirmation _____

Previous Community and Congregational Affiliation _____

_____

SPECIAL SKILLS, TALENTS and HOBBIES
(e.g. photography, baking, crafts)

_____

_____

FEMALE

Name _____

Hebrew Name (If applicable) _____

Date of Birth _____/_____/_____

Occupation _____

Business Name _____

Business Address _____

Business City & State _____ Zip Code _____

Business Telephone _____

RELIGIOUS BACKGROUND

☐ Reform ☐ Conservative ☐ Orthodox ☐ None

☐ Non Jewish (Religion Practiced) _____

☐ Convert to Judaism (year) _____

Date of Bat Mitzvah _____/_____/_____ Year of Confirmation _____

Previous Community and Congregational Affiliation _____

_____

SPECIAL SKILLS, TALENTS and HOBBIES
(e.g. photography, baking, crafts)

_____

_____

_____

DEPENDENT CHILDREN

Name	Hebrew Name	Birth Date	Attends rel. school List present grade

OTHER PERSONS IN HOUSEHOLD

Name	Relationship

I WOULD LIKE TO BE INVOLVED IN THE FOLLOWING

M F
☐ ☐ Adult Education
☐ ☐ Brotherhood
☐ ☐ Caring Community
☐ ☐ Choir
☐ ☐ Endowment
☐ ☐ Fund Raising
☐ ☐ Building
☐ ☐ Membership

M F
☐ ☐ Programming
☐ ☐ Publicity
☐ ☐ Religious School
☐ ☐ Ritual
☐ ☐ Sisterhood
☐ ☐ Social Action
☐ ☐ Hospitality
        Other _____

Memorials

Yahrzeits are observed and announced at that religious service closest to date of death. Please list names of those you wish remembered, their relationship to a specific family member, and the English month, day and year of death.

☐ I prefer to observe the Hebrew date.

_____

_____

_____

_____

_____

_____

Financial Commitment

The first quarterly payment of the dues and the first full year of Building Fund commitment must accompany this application. Religious School and Hebrew School fees must be paid before school registration. Dues bills will be sent quarterly. All financial obligations apply to the fiscal year which begins July 1st.

Signature(s)   X_____

of applicant(s)   X_____

Annual Dues .... $ _____
Religious School .... $ _____
Hebrew School .... $ _____
Building Fund .... $ _____
Initial Deposit .... $ _____
Balance .... $ _____

Building Fund

We (I) promise to pay to the order of Temple Jeremiah the sum of $ _____ payable in equal installments of $ _____ beginning on _____ 19____ and thereafter on July 1, 19____, July 1, 19____, July 1, 19____, July 1, 19____. The entire balance due shall be accelerated upon resignation or failure to renew membership in any year at Temple Jeremiah.

Signature (Husband) _____   Signature (Wife) _____

White - Personal File   Yellow - Member Copy

FOR OFFICE USE:

- -

COMP. _____CARDS _____COV. _____ YAHRZEIT _____LETTER-R _____LETTER-P _____

FIN. _____HHD. _____B/BM _____R.S. _____MEMB. LIST _____MENS. CHAIR. _____COFFEE _____

BIRTH. _____ANNIV._____

106

CONGREGANT INTEREST SURVEY

Name _____

If there is more than one adult at home, please indicate which Member of your household would like to paticipate in the following committees, auxiliaries and special projects by writing an "F" (Adult Female) and "M" (Adult Male) in the blank spaces below. If you are currently participating in any of the following activities, please indicate by placing an "X" in the blank spaces below.

COMMITTEES AND AUXILIARIES OF THE TEMPLE

_____ ART AND MUSEUM — Allocates funds and chooses ceremonial art and other Judaic art to enhance our facility.
Meetings: Usually monthly; may vary.

_____ BROTHERHOOD — Over 400 men providing service and educational programs to the Temple.

_____ Assist traffic flow in parking lot before and after Religious School.

_____ Assist as needed at the Jeannette and Jerome Cohen Retreat Center.

_____ Usher at Shabbat services on Friday evening and High Holidays.

_____ Video tape B'nai Mitzvah Ceremonies (training provided).

_____ Assist with the monthly Lunch with the Rabbi.

_____ Fundraising.

_____ BUILDING MAINTENANCE — Supervises the major maintenance needs of the Temple.
Meetings: Meets as necessary.

_____ CEMETERY — Supervises the care of the Rose Hill Cemetery, Rose Hill Mausoleum, and the B'nai Jehudah section in Elmwood Cemetery.
Meetings: Meets as necessary.

_____ COUPLES — "THIRTY-FORTY SOMETHING" — Provides program opportunities for couples to meet and socialize.
Meetings: Meets as necessary.

_____ EDUCATION — Sets goals and direction for the Temple Schools (Religious School, Hebrew School and Pre-School) and Adult Study programs in conjunction with the Rabbi/Educator.
Meetings: Monthly.

_____ EMPTY NESTERS — Provides program opportunities for couples and singles, age 50 plus, to become acquainted in a social setting.
Meetings: Meets as necessary.

_____ FRIENDLY VISITORS — Volunteers who regularly visit congregants in nursing homes and private homes. Assembles Shabbat and holiday packages and delivers them to Jewish residents in area nursing homes every other month.
Meetings: Sunday mornings, every other month.

_____ HAVURAH — Small groups of Temple members who are committed to enriching their Jewish lives through study, holiday celebrations, life cycle events and social sharing with other compatible members.
Meetings: Determined by individual Havurah.

_____ Yes, I am interested in joining a Havurah. I prefer a Havurah that is: (check all that apply)

_____ family oriented   _____ social   _____ study

_____ single members   _____ mixed age groups

_____ career oriented   _____ other: _____

                                                          _____ your age range

_____ "HELPING PROFESSIONALS" — Provides a variety of programs dealing with blended families, grief support, communication skills, self-esteem, and social and emotional growth to parents, children and teenagers in the congregation.
Meetings: Meets as necessary.

_____ LANDSCAPING — Supervises the care of the Temple lawns and shrubs.
Meetings: Meets as necessary.

_____ LEGAL — On call to handle the congregation's legal matters and to research the law as needed.
Prerequisite: Law Degree
Meetings: Meets as necessary.

_____ LIBRARY — Establishes policy for the operation and development of the Temple Library. Renders part-time assistance in the actual management of the Library.
Meetings: Twice a year.

_____ MEMBERSHIP INVOLVEMENT AND RECOGNITION — Welcomes new members with special gifts and programs and administers Volunteer Recognition program and Volunteer Recognition Shabbat.
Meetings: Meets as necessary.

_____ NEW MEMBER ACQUISITION — Stimulates interest in B'nai Jehudah among the unaffiliated. Meets with applicants for membership and assists them to complete the necessary forms.
Meetings: Meets as necessary.

_____ OUTREACH — Coordinates programs to integrate Jews-by choice and intermarried families into the congregation.
Meetings: Meets as necessary.

_____ PARA-RABBINICS — Helps members prepare for life cycle events and provides functions that would enhance, increase, and personalize the Congregation to the participants. Prerequisite: Requires special course of study.
Meetings: Meets as necessary.

_____ PUBLICITY — Volunteers are assigned to write press releases for the Temple Bulletin and Jewish Chronicle and/or design invitations, flyers, etc. for specific committees or events on a rotating basis.
Meetings: Meets as necessary.

_____ RELIGIOUS WORSHIP AND MUSIC — Plans in cooperation with the Rabbi's and Cantor, special and innovative worship and music programs, works to increase the attendance and participation of worship activities. Makes recommendations to the Board of any proposed changes in ritual.
Meetings: Monthly.

_____ SINGLES — Provides program opportunities, community service and service to the Congregation for single members of all ages to become acquainted and involved in the life of the congregation.
Meetings: Monthly.

_____ SISTERHOOD — Nearly 800 women who offer service and support to our congregation through a variety of programs.

_____ Serve lunch one Saturday a month for ATLAZ (seniors)

_____ Host students for AFS Shabbat Dinner and worship services.

_____ Assemble and serve meals for Project Restart (feeds hungry) on Sunday Mornings.

_____ Type materials for visually impaired.

_____ Assist with Religious School holiday celebrations.

_____ Prepare and serve for Kiddush luncheons.

_____ Prepare trays for weekly Oneg Shabbat.

_____ Bake for weekly Oneg Shabbat.

_____ Participate in Recruitment Telethons

_____ Fundraising events.

_____ Gift shop sales personnel.

_____ Plan programs for General Membership Meetings.

_____ SOCIAL JUSTICE — Involvement in social action activities on a local, national and international level. Programs and issues include hunger/food drives, blood drives, holiday toy drive, homelessness, AIDS, Ethiopian Jewry, Pro-Choice, Soviet Resettlement, Shomrei Adamah (environmental issues), Sanctuary.
Meetings: Monthly.

_____ VOLUNTEER CHOIR — Brings significant enhancement to the worship life of the Congregation. Only requirement is a love of singing.
Meetings: Weekly, Tuesday night rehearsal; and monthly participation at Friday Night Shabbat Service.

_____ YOUTH ACTIVITIES — Consists of several subcommittees which plan social and religious events for: (indicate if interested in the following)

____ Early Childhood   ____ Kindergarten-3rd Grade

____ 4th & 5th Grade   ____ Sixers (6th Grade)

____ JYG (7th-8th Grade)   ____ College (responsible for providing Judaic materials to and program for college youth).

____ TYG (9th-12th Grade)

Meetings: Every two months.

TEMPLE EVENTS

_____ Design age appropriate activities for High Holy Day Children's Program.

_____ Congregational Shabbat Dinners

_____ Congregational Sukkot Dinner and Festivities (October)

_____ Consecration Dinner (October)

_____ Jewish Book Month Activities for children and adults (November)

_____ Collect, sort, deliver toys for Holiday Toy Drive (December)

_____ Congregational "100 Menorah" Chanukah Dinner (December)

_____ Congregational Purim Dinner (February)

_____ Purim Carnival (February)

_____ Passover Second Night Seder (April)

_____ Israel Independence Day Celebration (May)

_____ Inter-racial Programs

_____ Family Weekend Retreat

OPPORTUNITIES FOR VOLUNTEER SERVICE TO THE TEMPLE
(Volunteer Activities which can be performed at the Temple:)

_____ Take photographs at Temple events: ____ I have my own camera.

_____ Assist with mailings; stuff envelopes, etc.

_____ Cook or prepare meals for Shabbat/Holiday dinners and/or special events.

_____ Serve meals for Shabbat/Holiday dinners and/or special events.

_____ Set tables for Shabbat/Holiday dinners and/or special events.

_____ Host/Hostess-greet and welcome members at Shabbat/Holiday dinners and/or special events.

_____ Registration (collect money, etc.) at dinner and/or special events.

_____ Assist in office (filing, typing, etc.)

_____ Assist in Library.

_____ Babysit for meetings, etc.

(Volunteer Activities which can be performed outside of Temple:)

_____ Design/create Table Decorations.

_____ Write publicity articles for Temple Bulletin and Jewish Chronicle for Congregational events.

_____ Design flyers/invitations for Congregational events.

_____ Make telephone calls.

_____ Typing

_____ Provide transportation to/from Temple for Shabbat/Holiday celebrations or special events.

_____ Provide transportation for the elderly or newly arrived Russian emigre families for doctor appointments, shopping, etc.

_____ Sell ads for a Temple publication.

....

_____ Host congregants in our home for: Number of persons_____

_____ Shabbat Dinner

_____ Rosh Hashanah

_____ Yom Kippur Break the Fast

_____ Dinner in our Sukkah

_____ Passover Seder   _____ 1st Night   _____ 2nd Night

_____ If you would like to be invited as a guest to any of the above Shabbat/Holiday home celebrations, please mark a "G" in the above spaces.   Number of _____ Adults   _____ Children

_____ Serve as host family to a newly arrived Russian emigre family.

....

_____ Do you have any special talents and/or hobbies you would be willing to offer and share with the Congregation?

Please list: _____

_____

_____

_____

_____ Have you heard of or been involved in activities in your business, or in another community that you think were very successful which could be implemented at the Temple? Please give a brief description:

_____

_____

_____

_____

_____

_____

_____ Your additional comments would be most appreciated.

_____

_____

_____

_____

_____

_____

_____

PLEASE RETURN THIS SURVEY ALONG WITH YOUR PERSONAL DATA FORM IN THE ENCLOSED ENVELOPE.

THANK YOU.

(The Temple Congregation B'nai Jehudah, Kansas City, MO)

Volunteer Interest Form

To: _____

From: Annette Fish (363-1050)
          Program Coordinator

_____ has recently indicated
              (Name)

an interest in _____.
                    (committee or special project)

Would you please contact _____

at _____ to discuss this further.
        (phone number)

I would appreciate follow-up feedback from you. Thank you for your

cooperation.

Additional Comments: _____

_____

_____

_____

- -

_____   I have contacted _____

_____   Please add to my committee/project roster

_____   Additional Comments: _____

_____

_____

_____   _____
      Your Signature   Date

(The Temple Congregation B'nai Jehudah, Kansas City, MO)

111

ADULT EDUCATION

PLEASE NOTE DATE CHANGES

Feeling at Home in the Temple

A series of six sessions that will answer the following dilemmas

- Why am I a Jew?
- What do I tell my relatives about Reform Judaism?
- Do I have to defend myself against Conservative and Orthodox criticism?
- Help, the prayerbook is Greek to me

Get acquainted with the Temple. Get to know Rabbi Stroh, Cantor Steinhouse, Rabbi Gottlieb and other local Rabbis.

Meet and make friends with members, some, just as new as you are.

October 18	Introduction to Judaism
November 1	Reform Practice
November 8	Prayer Book
November 15	Shabbat and Holidays
November 22	Service Melodies
November 29	Life Cycle

Thursday evenings at the Temple – 8:00pm

(Temple Har Zion, Thornhill, Ontario, Canada)

112

NEW MEMBERS SHABBAT

Temple Shalom invites your family

to be our honored guests

for Shabbat Dinner

on October 19, 1990, at 6:30 p.m.

Dinner will be followed by our

annual New Members Shabbat Service

during which presentations will be made

to each new family, to welcome you to

Temple Shalom

NEW MEMBERS SHABBAT   **OCTOBER 19, 1990**

The _____ Family
will _____ attend the New Members Shabbat Dinner
and Service.
Number of Family Members who will attend: _____
_____ would like to read a portion of the service in:
English _____ Hebrew _____
Please reply by October 8th. to Sharon Rosner
19 Burnham Place, Flanders, New Jersey 07836
927-0027

(Temple Shalom, Succasunna, NJ)

113

NEW MEMBERS WELCOME

RABBI:

Baruch ha-ba b'shem Adonai. Blessed are those who come in
God's name. Berachnuchem mi'bet Adonai. May you be blessed
in and out of God's house.

NEW MEMBERS:

We have come to this sanctuary to become part of a community.
We have come to join with people who believe that the world
rests on Torah, worship and deeds of lovingkindness. As
we are one in worship in this congregation, so may we remain
as one, together serving God with all our heart, all our soul
and all our might.

TOGETHER:

Our God and God of our ancestors, help us to realize the
unity of Your Creation.   As You are one, so must our lives
be one. May the integrity of our lives reflect Your Oneness,
wherever we are, whatever we do.

May we never be guilty of affirming You in this sanctuary only
to deny You elsewhere. Help us to know when our lives are
contradictions, when we war with ourselves and with others,
when we undo the good we have done.

May we be wholehearted in revering You, O God.

Remove from us all that is hateful: bring us near to all that
You love. May our search for sanctity as a kingdom of priests
and a holy people continue, morning and evening, all the days
of our lives. And let us say: Amen.

CANTOR AND CONGREGATION:

Shehechianu

(Temple Sinai, Summit, NJ)

114

JEWISH COMMUNITY CENTER
BULLETIN

Volume 41, No. 1 • 1 Elul 5749 • **September 1, 1989** • White Plains, N.Y.

N.M.N. ???

The N.M.N. is the New Members Network, composed of families and single people who joined J.C.C. during 1988 and 1989. All our new members, who want to make new friends and become involved in Temple life, are invited to become part of the New Members Network (NMN).

Why N.M.N? Some new members who want to participate in Temple life, find it difficult to get started. So we addressed this issue! Under Ruth Lusk's able leadership, a Steering Committee evolved, brainstormed and finally a first gathering. The Steering Committee contacted all new members and the response from the "Class of 1988 and 1989" was impressive! About 70 new members, of all ages, attended one of five gatherings—all held on a summer Saturday evening (August 5th), and hosted by couples from the Steering Committee: Julie and Ron Carran joined with Susan Strickler and Richard Kaye, Renee and Steve Cohen, Bonnie and Eric Eilen, Sandy and Alan Seckular joined with Janet and Mark Hershey and Betty Birenbach was assisted by Anita and Stanley Goodman.

How does N.M.N. function? All new members are called by the Steering Committee members and are invited to attend services and special Temple events. Our next event: a Family Picnic with games and fun activities for all ages. The date: Sunday, September 24th, starting at 12:30 P.M.

Later in the year the current Steering Committee will relinquish its role to the "Class of 1989-90": and N.M.N. will perpetuate itself. But most important, our new members will have established ties to JCC and reinforced them with new friendships.

SECTION C. RETENTION

This section contains suggestions
and programmatic ideas for
involving members, making the
most of meeetings, creating a
sense of community and
responding to the changing needs
of temple membership.

RETENTION

Membership retention is not a one-time program that you can implement or a new committee that you can form. Membership retention is the culmination of a process that begins with recruitment and continues with a program of integration. Membership retention involves responding to the changing needs of your membership, creating a sense of community within the congregation, and involving members in all stages of their lives. It means running the congregation in an efficient, effective and congenial manner. Membership retention demands the creation of a vital congregation in which membership is meaningful — giving your members a reason to belong — touching congregants in a significant way and making Judaism an important facet of their lives.

I. INVOLVING TEMPLE MEMBERS

* Maintain a Skills Bank of members' skills and interests

* Call on congregants to become involved in a particular event or for a short-term project rather than always inviting them to on-going committee meetings

* Assign a staff member as the "Volunteer Coordinator" to oversee volunteer activities and provide support and supervision for volunteers

* Train volunteers and lay leaders for their tasks

* Don't reinvent the wheel with each changeover in leadership; create a system in which information is passed from one chair to his/her successor

* Recognize volunteers for their work

    — The Social Action Committee of Temple Emanu El (Houston, TX) has a Volunteer Appreciation Luncheon each year for all those who work on its various projects

    — Temple Sinai (Sharon, MA) has a Volunteer Shabbat each year to honor volunteers; one year each volunteer received a Temple Sinai mug with a note of thanks, the next year they each received a perennial plant (volunteers should keep coming back like these plants).

    — Like many congregations, Temple David (Monroeville, PA) has a Wall of Honor — but theirs is a bit different. One side is for those who donate money, the other side is for those who have given substantially of their time and effort in volunteer projects.

    — Temple B'nai Jehudah (Kansas City, MO) has instituted a Volunteer Recognition *Avodah* (Service) Award which members earn by tracking their service hours to the congregation. All volunteers receive recognition at a Volunteer Recognition Shabbat. Those who earn 100 hours or more are invited as the congregation's guests to a special Shabbat dinner before the services and receive a special certificate. The three volunteers who accumulate the most hours in a given year receive special honors at the dinner and service, and recognition in the Temple Bulletin and local Jewish paper.

* Encourage all members to observe home rituals and to enrich their Judaism

    — require Board members to take a Basic Judaism class

    — provide opportunities for the entire congregation to learn more about basic Jewish practices, observances, etc.

    — use the Temple Bulletin as a vehicle for teaching, i.e, print the Chanukah blessings with translations and transliterations

    — encourage members to prepare *divrei Torah* for committee meetings

II. MAKING THE MOST OF MEETINGS

* Conduct all meetings as efficiently as possible; don't waste your members' volunteer time

* Instill a sense of purpose in your meetings, connect them to the purpose of your synagogue

  — begin *all* meetings with a short *d'var Torah*

  — refer back to your Mission Statement on occasion as a point of reference for your activities

* Arrange for a Leadership Development Training Program (sponsored by the UAHC Department of Synagogue Management) for temple board members and committee chairs

* Congregation Emanu El (Houston, TX) has most committees meet on the same night. Supper is served at a nominal charge prior to the meetings. This provides an opportunity for congregants to come together as a community. Including supper makes it easier for people to attend the meetings

* Have an annual Board retreat at the beginning of the congregational year to allow Board members, especially new ones, the opportunity to become acquainted, to focus on philosophical issues of the congregation, to set goals and objectives for the year, and to have *fun.*

III. CREATING A SENSE OF COMMUNITY

* Encourage congregants to make formal commitments to involvement in the congregation

  — Monmouth Reform Temple (Tinton Falls, NJ) has created the "Mitzvot of Membership" that addresses the commitment expected of members in the areas of study, worship and community. Members are encouraged to make a spiritual pledge during the High Holy Days. (See text in Integration section)

  — At Temple B'nai Tikvah (Calgary, Alberta, Canada) members pledge *mitzvot* instead of money on Yom Kippur.

* Have a mini "town meeting" in addition to the annual meeting to allow congregants to speak about their concerns in a friendly and relaxed atmosphere.

* Organize a congregational retreat in which congregants can study, play and share Shabbat together in an informal atmosphere. Larger congregations can organize different retreats for smaller groups from within the congregation.

* For Medium and Large Congregations - organize *chavurot* (small friendship groups) in which congregants can meet, study, socialize and celebrate together in smaller grups within the congregation.

IV. RESPONDING TO THE CHANGING NEEDS OF TEMPLE MEMBERSHIP

Congregants will remain a part of your congregation if they have a good reason to stay. By developing programs which respond to the various needs of your membership, you enable congregants to grow Jewishly and make meaningful connections.

1. Conduct a needs assessment of your congregation to determine the direction you will take (See samples in this section). In this survey you will need to learn

   * basic demographic information
   * religious background
   * geographic distribution of congregation
   * members' interests

120

* what members would like to see at temple

Some helpful statistics to know for program development are the percent of your membership that is

— Single (35 and under)
— Young marrieds
— Pre-school families
— Religious School families
— Single parents
— Singles (over 35)
— Post-Confirmation families
— Seniors
— Interfaith Families
— New Jews by Choice

2. Developing Programmatic Responses

Once you determine who is in your congregation and what particular needs they have that are in consonance with your mission statement, you can begin to develop appropriate programs. It would be impossible to list all successful program ideas for the different populations within a congregation. The suggestions included below are the more "unusual" synagogue programs that particularly help to create a sense of community within the congregation and respond to needs which are often overlooked in synagogues.

Please call your regional director and refer to *The Guide: A Directory of the Programs, Services and Resources of the Union of American Hebrew Congregations and the Reform Movement* (available through the UAHC Program Department) for additional ideas. For *Young Adult* and *Early Childhood* programming ideas, see the Recruitment Section of this book.

A. Caring Community Activities

* Develop a "Caring Community" Committee to help the congregation meet the personal needs of its members, particularly to fulfill such *mitzvot* as comforting the bereaved and visiting the sick. Use the Temple Bulletin and/or Shabbat services as vehicles to ask congregants to let the temple know when members are seriously ill or suffer a personal tragedy.

* The *Reyut* (Friendship) Committee of Vassar Temple (Poughkeepsie, NY), acts as a "friend in need" for congregants who suffer losses, are ill, or who have other difficulties. In addition, they offer a special service to congregants: if working parents have a child who becomes ill and no one is available to stay home, a committee member will step in to help. It is understood that the person will return the service if possible.

* Members of Congregation Emanu El (Houston, TX) formed an AIDS Care Team to help care for people with AIDS, both in the congregation and in the community.

* Establish support groups, facilitated by trained individuals, social workers and/or rabbis for different needs, such as bereavement, cancer patients and survivors, caretaker's and loved ones of Alzheimer's patients, widow/widowers, remarried couples, single parents and the like. (See the examples of Temple Israel, West Bloomfiled, MI and Congregation Beth Israel, Houston, TX)

* Congregation Shir Tikvah (Troy, MI) instituted a "Dial-A-Shofar" program that allows shut-ins to hear a taped rendition of the shofar service during the High Holy Days.

* Congregation Emanu El (Houston, TX) offers homebound individuals the opportunity to participate in Friday Evening and Holy Day worship services through a telephone hookup.

B. Congregation-wide activities

* Religious School class Shabbat dinners preceeding services

* Especially for Small Congregations -Congregation Kol Havarim (Glastonbury, CT) runs a monthly *kabbalat Shabbat,* in which all interested congregants join for a pot-luck dinner in someone's home to welcome Shabbat in a relaxed, casual atmosphere.

* Temple Beth-El (San Antonio, TX) holds a Passover Dessert Seder on the seventh night of Passover. A modified Haggadah is used and a religious school class is responsible for hosting the evening and presenting a program. An average of 250-300 members attend.

* Temple Kol Ami (West Bloomfield, MI) holds holiday workshops for adults about two weeks prior to different holidays during the year. Upon enrolling, each person or couple is issued an empty binder that they fill at each session with packets containing blessings, songs with sheet music, background on history and observances, recipes, reading lists and activities for children. The workshops involve a variety of learning and experiential activities.

* The Young People's Congregation of Anshe Chesed Fairmount Temple (Beachwood, OH) invites families to bring any children born in the last year to Shavuot services for a special blessing of their "first fruits".

C. Programming for Teenagers

One of the most common times for members to leave congregations is after their youngest child becomes a Bar or Bat Mitzvah. It goes without saying that one of the ways we can encourage these families to remain in the congregation is by involving their children. As children grow into young adults, the experiences they have in their congregation will also affect their desire to affiliate when they are on their own.

* Congregation Shir Tikvah (Troy, MI) has a pre-teen group which "graduates" a class into their NFTY group each year. The pre-Confirmation program is an experiential one with no classroom or texts, but filled with field trips, audio-visual programs and the like. The congregation has also established a special *teen membership* for those instances where the young adults want to remain involved despite the families' departure from the congregation.

* The Reform congregations in the Bergen County area of New Jersey band together for their post-Bar Mitzvah classes. BARJ (Bergen Academy of Reform Judaism) students meet young people from other synagogues and participate in a retreat and *shabbaton* each year. BARJ is open to unaffiliated teens as well.

* Temple Beth Tikvah (Wayne, NJ) invites children to particiate in the Haftorah readings during the High Holy Days in the year immediately after they become B'nai Mitzvah.

* Congregation Bet Breira (Miami, FL) presents all of its confirmands with a ten-year free membership in the congregation which gives them a strong message that they are wanted in the community.

D. Adult education programs

* Temple Emeth (Teaneck, NJ) offers an "Adult Confirmation Class", which involves a year-long program of study with the rabbi about Judaism, Jewish

history and Reform Judaism, learning prayerbook Hebrew with the Cantor, undertaking a personal service project for the synagogue or community, and creating and participating in a special service following Shavuot to affirm participants' mature commitment to Judaism and the Jewish People.

* Temple Israel (West Bloomfield, MI) offers an Adult Affirmation program for its members which involves completing a required number of adult education hours through participation in the temple's study programs or in other acceptable courses.

E. Seniors Programming

* Emanu Elders of Congregation Emanu El (Houston, TX), which is under the auspices of the Sisterhood, provides a wide range of activities for its members, including a monthly social action project for the local food pantry and an annual retreat at the Greene Family Camp.

* A number of congregations on Long Island have "Chai Clubs" for those who have been members for 18 years or more. Each of the Chai Clubs has a variety of social, educational and cultural activites as well as joint activities during the year. (Suburban Temple, Wantagh, NY is an example)

* "New Horizons", a seniors group at Temple Sholom (Chicago, IL) has a variety of activities, including a monthly Shabbat dinner before services.

MEMBERSHIP PHONE SURVEY

Guidelines:

As leaders of your congregation, members of the Board of Trustees can play a vital role in membership retention. It should be seen, in fact, as part of their responsibility. When Board members connect personally with members of the congregation once a year for no other reason than to extend a holiday greeting and to find out how things are going, that sends a strong message of caring and concern. In addition, such contact can give Board members important information on the overall functioning of the congregation. For instance, when several elderly members comment that they would attend services more frequently if they had transportation, it becomes clear that there is an important member need that is not being met and steps can be taken to correct the situation. Members then feel appreciated and cared for in a deeper way than if the temple response were made after a complaint and they are able to continue to participate more fully in temple life.

Hints for Implementation:

1. Set aside a particular season each year to make calls, for instance just before Pesach. Allow enough time (1 month) for the calls to be made, but do include a deadline.

2. This program has the greatest benefit when all members of the Board, including officers, participate. Divide the membership list among the trustees so that no one person has too many people to call. It may be necessary because of the relatively large size of your membership or the small size of your Board to contact only half of the membership each year.

3. Do not combine this phone contact with any solicitation of funds.

4. When explaining the project to members of the Board, model or role play a typical call, as they may feel awkward about initiating the conversation.

   "Hello, Sam. This is Ruth Adler. I'm calling on behalf of the Board of Trustees of Temple to wish you a good Passover and just to ask how things are going....The Temple values your membership and participation and we are very interested to know if we are meeting your needs."

   Personalize the call if you can: "Hi, Sam. This is Ruth. I'm calling with my Board 'hat' on, officially to wish you a happy Pesach and to ask how you're feeling about your participation at Temple. Is there anything we could be doing that we're not?" or "I know you just joined the temple last year. How are things going? Did you know the Young Couples Club is going to see 'Fiddler' next Saturday night? I'll have Vicky call you with the particulars if you'd like to go."

   Follow your own style. Some people like a humorous touch: "No, I'm not calling to ask you for money, simply to wish you a very sweet Pesach...."

5. Reassure Board members that the calls do not take a great deal of time, that most members are very pleasantly surprised and pleased to have been called, and that the calls are extremely important in creating the kind of atmosphere your congregation is striving for. It means a lot to members to receive a personal call from a Board of Trustees member.

6. Timely follow-up is extremely important. When suggestions or needs are elicited, we create the expectation of a response which must be met. Assign one person the responsibility of follow-up. That person should receive all response sheets, note all instances where follow-up is necessary and make sure that the proper person, whether the rabbi, the president or some other committee chair, is made aware of the need for response. In most instances, a phone call is all that is required.

SAMPLE LETTER TO BOARD OF TRUSTEES FOR MEMBERSHIP PHONE SURVEY

March 1, 1991

Dear Member of the Board of Trustees:

Temple Temple rightly prides itself on being a warm, welcoming congregation, one that cares for its members as part of an extended family and encourages participation. Most of us do indeed experience Temple Temple in that way. But as leaders of a congregation of about 450 individuals and families, we bear the responsibility for nurturing our family and providing the opportunity for every member to find his/her own place.

In order to foster connection for our members and to sharpen our hearing of their concerns, the Membership Committee is once again requesting each of you to make several calls in the next three weeks. So that the task will not be too onerous, we will be contacting only half of the congregation at this time. Please make every effort to speak with everyone on your list.

What to say and how to say it? Your own informal conversational style is perfect. (In other words, don't read off a list of questions!) We want to accomplish the following goals:

* communicating that you are calling because, as a trustee, you care about her/him/them and their experience at Temple Temple and you want to hear their views. (This may be all that's needed.)

* learning whether Temple Temple is meeting their needs and if not, what they would like.

* letting them know about upcoming temple events they might be interested in. (Keep the March calendar by the phone while you are calling.)

Above all, be a warm, personal contact whom they can speak with about any part of temple life. Wish them a Happy Passover.

IMPORTANT: Please note briefly both positive and negative comments, as well as suggestions on your response sheet. Put a *BIG RED STAR* next to any item that requires attention. It is extremely important that an immediate response be made to any problem. The Membership Committee will follow up.

Response sheets should be returned by Thursday, APRIL 5 to me at (HOME ADDRESS) or to my box at the temple. Call me in the evening at 123-4567 if you encounter problems. Thank you in advance for all your efforts.

Judah Maccabee
Membership Retention

Temple Temple Membership Canvas
1991- 5751

Name of Board Member: _____

_____

Temple Member	Date Called	Comments

CONGREGATION PHONE EXIT POLL
Instructions

When a member submits a letter of resignation or does not renew his/her membership, it is extremely important for someone from the congregation to contact that person,

* first, to find out why the person is leaving and explore ways to enable the person to remain with the congregation;
* and second, to learn from members' dissatisfaction about areas of congregational life that need improvement.

Both objectives can be met with one phone call. Phone calls should be made as soon as possible after a resignation has been received to demonstrate the concern of the congregation for the member. The calls should be made by someone with authority in the temple, someone who knows the overall programming, activities, etc., usually a member of the board of directors or the executive committee or, where appropriate, the rabbi. In some congregations, a member of the membership committee may be assigned this task.

In any cases in which a person expresses anger or dissatisfaction with a particular staff member or committee, such feelings should be made known to the appropriate person immediately.

Using the attached "Guidelines for the Phone Exit Poll" and the Exit Poll will help you to learn more about your congregation and areas which might be in need of improvement. These tools are designed as models and may be adapted for your own needs.

Follow-up: In general, the exit polls should be collected and summarized periodically by a board member or member of the membership committee. The results of the polls should be presented to the Board and actions taken where needed.

GUIDELINES FOR THE PHONE EXIT POLL

Before making the phone call, be sure to have the following at hand:

1. the person's membership form (which should be read through before the phone call)

2. the member's letter of resignation (if available)

3. the attached Exit Poll

4. pen and paper for note-taking

When making the phone call:

1. Introduce yourself and say that you understand that they have decided to resign from the temple.

2. Indicate your concern about their resignation, ask for their reasons and explore if anything can be done to change their mind.

3. Explain that their criticisms are important to you and their responses will help you try to improve temple life. (Even if they won't reconsider their resignation, their comments can help you improve temple for others.)

4. Refer to the information needed for the Exit Poll and ask them to evaluate the various areas outlined. Take general notes while you are speaking with the person and fill in the Exit Poll *after* your conversation.

5. Fill in as much of the demographic information as you can before making the call and ask for any additional information needed at the end of the conversation.

6. It is very important to promise confidentiality.

7. KEEP YOUR TONE FRIENDLY AND OPEN; DO NOT BE PATRONIZING OR DEFENSIVE. Be prepared for the possibility of speaking to a very angry person.

8. Thank the person for his/her time and openness. Reiterate how important their input has been.

UAHC Task Force on the Unaffiliated

CONGREGATION _____ EXIT POLL

1. Demographic information:

   A. Member (name and age): _____

   B. Spouse, if applicable (name and age): _____

   C. Minor children, if applicable name(s) and age(s): _____

   _____

   D. Adult children (married or single) living in our community:

   Name   Age

   Children belong to: _____   our congregation

                           _____   another congregation

                           _____   no congregation

   E. Member's future plans:

      1. definite plan to join another congregation _____

      2. planning not to affiliate at all with another congregation _____

2. Temple Services and Programs

   (Use the following rating scale: E = excellent, G = good, F = fair or P = poor)

                     Religious school _____

                     Hebrew School _____

                     Adult Education _____

                     Rabbinic Services _____

                     Worship Services _____

                     High Holy Days _____

                     Dues Program _____

                     Nursery School _____

                     Social Functions _____

                     Programs for Older Members _____

3. List the areas the member indicated as poor and the reasons for the member's dissatisfaction:

4. Additional comments and criticisms:

Complete the following data before making the call.

1. Date filled out: _____

2. Poll conducted by: _____

3. Member or family polled: _____

   Phone number: _____

4. Date joined congregation: _____ Date resigned: _____

5. Was a letter sent by the family to the congregation indicating that they are resigning?

   _____

6. If yes, what reasons(s) did the member indicate for resigning?

   _____

TEMPLE ISAIAH MEMBERSHIP UPDATE CENSUS

Over the past few years, our membership has grown by leaps
and bounds. For each of us the years have brought changes in
family size, e.g. births, deaths, marriages, divorce, etc.
In order to make our Temple a more caring community, we need
to determine the needs of our congregants and to develop both
individual and group support services for our membership.
A current priority of the Union of American Hebrew
Congregations is the development of "Caring Congregational
Communities". The Board of Trustees of Temple Isaiah believe
that this should be a top priority of our congregation.

The first task we face is to open lines of communications
with our congregation. For this reason we want to know more
about you, and ask your cooperation in filling out this
questionnaire.

PLEASE RETURN BY :   IMMEDIATELY !!!

(Temple Isaiah, Lexington, MA)

131

1. NAME_____TITLE _____

2. I am Jewish, by birth_____conversion_____I am not Jewish
   and ___ I practice another faith_____do not practice
   another faith.

3. Home address_____
   _____

4. Home telephone_____

5. Birthdate_____

6. Business/Profession_____

7. Business title_____

8. Business address_____
   _____

9. Business phone_____

10. Are you retired?_____

11. Extent of religious training:
    Bar/Bat Mitzvah_____Confirmation_____Hebrew High School
    _____Youth Group___NFTY____USY____other_____

12. Can you:
    read Hebrew_____ speak Hebrew_____lead services_____
    sing in choir_____chant/read Torah, Haftorah_____
    chant Kiddush_____ bless candles_____
    Have you ever taught in a religious school ?_____
    Where_____
    When_____ How long_____

13. I am married_____ not married_____ divorced_____
    separated_____ widow/widower_____

14. Name of Spouse_____

15. Wedding anniversary date_____

16. Are your parents living?_____mother_____father_____
    Do they live in Lexington/area?_____ With you?_____
    In a nursing home?_____Address_____

17. Number of years you have lived in Lexington/area_____

18. Please list your special talents and/or interests and how
    you feel you might contribute to the Isaiah community?
    _____
    _____
    _____

QUESTIONS 19-35 FOR SPOUSE:

19. Name_____Title_____

20. I am Jewish, by birth_____conversion_____I am not Jewish
    and ___ I practice another faith_____do not practice
    another faith.

21. Birthdate_____

22. Business/Profession_____

23. Business title_____

24. Business address_____
    _____

25. Business phone_____

26. Are you retired?_____

27. Extent of religious training:
    Bar/Bat Mitzvah_____Confirmation_____Hebrew High School
    _____Youth Group___NFTY____USY____other_____

28. Can you:
    read Hebrew_____ speak Hebrew_____lead services_____
    sing in choir_____chant/read Torah, Haftorah_____
    chant Kiddush_____ bless candles_____
    Have you ever taught in a religious school ?_____
    Where_____
    When_____ How long_____

29. Are your parents living?____mother_____father_____
    Do they live in Lexington/area?_____ With you?_____
    In a nursing home?_____Address_____
30. Number of years you have lived in Lexington/area_____
31. Please list your special talents and/or interests and how
    you feel you might contribute to the Isaiah community?
    _____
    _____
    _____

32. Children (single)   Living at
    Name_____Birthdate_____ home?___
                                                         Living at
    Name_____Birthdate_____ home?___
                                                         Living at
    Name_____Birthdate_____ home?___
                                                         Living at
    Name_____Birthdate_____ home?___
                                                         Living at
    Name_____Birthdate_____ home?___

33. Children(married)
    Name_____Spouse's name_____
    Birthdate_____Birthdate_____
    Address_____
    Names of grandchildren_____
    _____
    Name_____Spouse's name_____
    Birthdate_____Birthdate_____
    Address_____
    Names of grandchildren_____
    _____
    Name_____Spouse's name_____
    Birthdate_____Birthdate_____
    Address_____
    Names of grandchildren_____
    _____

34. Other relatives living in household_____
    Name_____Relation_____Birthdate___
    Name_____Relation_____Birthdate___
    Name_____Relation_____Birthdate___
    Name_____Relation_____Birthdate___
    Name_____Relation_____Birthdate___
35. Are any members living in your household disabled or
    physically impaired? _____
    (If we are to meet the needs of these members, we need to
    be aware of such things as deafness, vision impairment or
    use of wheelchairs,etc.)
    Name_____Disability/Impairment_____
    Name_____Disability/Impairment_____
    Name_____Disability/Impairment_____
36. Year of affiliation with Temple Isaiah_____
37. Prior affiliation:
              Reform   Conservative   Orthodox   None
    Self   _____   _____   _____   ____
    Spouse   _____   _____   _____   ____
38. Yahrzeits:(only if you have not previously provided us
    with this information)
    Name: Do you observe Hebrew date? English date?
                                                                    133
    _____   _____

---------------------   ----------------   ----------------
---------------------   ----------------   ----------------
---------------------   ----------------   ----------------

39. Are there any support services that you would be interested in giving or sharing with other members of Temple Isaiah?_____
_____
40. Have you any suggestions for group programming?
_____
_____
_____

41.   COMMITTEE(S) SERVICE REQUESTS
     Please signify yor preference for committee service by
                 marking the appropriate boxes.

ADULT EDUCATION (programs include lectures, study groups, panel discussions, etc.)member_____ spouse_____
BEREAVEMENT (assists family in crisis at time of death of family member)   member_____ spouse _____
CHOIR (sings at various services during the year)
                             member_____ spouse_____
COMMITTEE ON AGING (liason to elderly services in area)
                             member_____ spouse_____
EDUCATION (determines policies of religious school,employs teachers ,makes recommendations) member_____spouse____
HIGH HOLY DAYS (tickets, seating, etc.)
                             member_____ spouse_____
HOUSE (oversees property/building maintenance and improvements.)   member_____ spouse_____

LIBRARY (responsible for organizing and staffing)
                             member_____ spouse_____
MEMBERSHIP (membership acquisition, retention,recommendations to Board)   member_____ spouse_____
MEMBERSHIP LIASON (encourage new member participation)
                             member_____ spouse_____
RITUAL COMMITTEE (ceremonial arrangements, events for religious services in conjunction with Rabbi)
                             member_____ spouse_____
SOCIAL ACTION (informs Board and recommends re: current human relations problems)   member_____ spouse_____
YOUTH COMMITTEE (promote the welfare of the Congregation's children, socially and culturally / assists in coordination and development of Temple youth activities)
                             member_____ spouse_____
43. Are you a current member of :
                    Sisterhood_____ ,Brotherhood_____

THANK YOU FOR YOUR COOPERATION!!!!!!!!!!!!!!!!!!!!!!!!!!!!!!!!

PLEASE USE THE ENCLOSED STAMPED ENVELOPE AND RETURN
                    IMMEDIATELY

134

CONGREGATION EMANU EL
Houston, Texas
SURVEY

PERSONAL INFORMATION

Please answer the following questions by marking the item that best describes you.

Age	Sex	Marital Status	Family & Friends
_20-25	_Female	_Single	_ Large Family in Houston
_26-30	_Male	_Married without children	_ Small Family in Houston
_31-35		_Married with children	_ No Family in Houston
_36-40		_Divorced without children	_ Large group of friends
_over 40		_Divorced with children	_ Samll group of friends
		_Widowed without children	_ No friends
		_Widowed with children	
		_Partner in a long-term relationship	

Birthplace
_ Houston
_ Other city in Texas
_ Other State

Previous City of Residence
_ Always lived in Houston
_ Moved to Houston from

_____

Occupation: Check more than one, but please specify
_Professional _____
_Sales _____
_Financial _____
_Arts_____
_Business _____
_Homemaker _____
_Vounteer _____
_Other _____

ACTIVITY INTERESTS

What kinds of activities would you like to see offered by the Temple for you?

_____

_____

_____

If we offered the following programs, which would you attend? You may check more than one, but be sure it is something you would do, not just something in which you are interested.

Cultural
_Theater
_Symphony
_Ballet
_Opera
_Jazz
_Museums
_Movies
_Other

Sports
(Spectator)
_Football/Oilers
_Basketball/Rockets
_Baseball/Astros
(Participating)
_Golf
_Tennis
_Running
_Walking
_Cycling
_Other

Social
_Country/Western Evening
_Comedy Club
_Game Night
_Dinner/Dancing
_Day Trips

Intellectual Activities
__Lectures
__Movies
__Discussion Groups
__Other

Spiritual Activities
__Worship Services
__Study Groups
__Classes
__Interfaith Groups
__Retreats

Social Action Activities
Caring for or assiting the
__Blind
__Children
__Elderly
__AIDs Patients
Working or Helping at
__Hospitals
__S.E.A.R.C.H.
__Home Repair
__Food Pantry
__Clothing Center
__Other

GROUP COMPOSITION

This deals with the make-up of the group with which you would like to participate. You may indicate more than one.

I like to be with people who are:
__ Age 20-25
__ Age 25-30
__ Age 20-30
__ Age 25-35
__ Age 35-40
__ Over 40
__ Doesn't Matter
__ Only Singles
__ Only Marrieds
__ Marrieds & Singles
__ People with children
__ Only Females
__ Only Males
__ Male & Female
__ Out of school and working

TIME COMMITMENT
__ Once a week   __ Once a month   __ Every other month
__ Three times yearly   __ Four times yearly __ Depends on program offered

Amount of Money you would spend:
   On a regular basis:
   __ Less than $25 per event
   __ Between $25-35 per event
   __ Between $25-50 per event

   One Time Events:
   __ Less than $25
   __ Between $25-35
   __ Between $25-50

136

Introduction

Dear Congregant:

The Human Resources within our Congregation comprise our most important asset. The members of our synagogue bring the greatest strengths, skills, and insights into our midst. How can we identify these resources; respond to them; involve them; and benefit from them? Our Human Resources Committee is endeavoring to find the answers. Please, help us.

The following questionnaire is divided into three parts:

1.   Our membership profile

2.   Expansion & development of our program

3.   Individual participation

Please, complete this and send it to us. We shall respond to your input as quickly and appropriately as possible.

Thank you for your help.

Chairperson,
Human Resources Committee

Part One   Human Resources Profile

NAME: _____

ADDRESS: _____

_____

HOME PHONE: _____   BUSINESS PHONE: _____

PROFESSION: _____

Special Skills/Interests/Hobbies	Level of Proficiency (check x)		
	Participate	Advanced	Can Teach
_____	_____	_____	_____
_____	_____	_____	_____
_____	_____	_____	_____

SPOUSE: _____

Profession: _____   Business phone: _____

Special Skills/Interests/Hobbies	Levels of Proficiency (check x)		
	Participate	Advanced	Can Teach
_____	_____	_____	_____
_____	_____	_____	_____
_____	_____	_____	_____

CHILDREN:

NAME: _____ AGE: ____   GRADE: ____   SEX: ___

_____ ____   ____   ____

Special Skills/Interests/Hobbies	Levels of Proficiency (check x)		
	Participate	Advanced	Can Teach
_____	_____	_____	_____
_____	_____	_____	_____
_____	_____	_____	_____

Please, use reverse side, if necessary ...

Part Two   Expansion & Development of
Our Program

What types of programs would you like to see in our congregation? We've listed just a few areas to stimulate thought.

<u>AREA</u>   <u>PROGRAM SUGGESTION</u>

Adult Education
Special Small Interest Groups
Family Programming
Special Programs for Single Parents
Special Programs for Singles
Special Programs for the Elderly
Special Interest Hobby Groups
Congregational Trips & Outings
Joint Parent/Child Education
Additional Worship Services
Havdalah Hour
Outreach

_____

_____ _____

_____ _____

_____

Please use the back of this page to explain your suggestions.

... continued on next page

Part Three   Individual Participation

The following is a list of our congregation's committees. On which committee would you be interested in serving? Remember to indicate the respective person(s).

__ Worship
__ Music & Choir
__ Festival Services
__ Daily Services
__ Special Services
__ Ushering
__ Festival Celebrations
__ Religious Education
__ Youth Activities
__ Adult Education
__ Youth Awards
__ Nursery School
__ Fund Raising
__ Budget
__ House
__ Personnel
__ _____
__ _____

__ Social Action
__ Inter-faith
__ Life Cycle
__ Family Programming
__ Havurot
__ 40 + singles
__ Young Congregants
__ Library
__ Alumnae
__ Public Relations
__ Constitution
__ Legal
__ Cemetery
__ Endowments
__ Membership
__ Dues & Assessment
__ _____
__ _____

Are there areas of congregational life other than committees in which you would like to become involved? Please explain. _____
_____
_____

If time commitment is a problem, would you be prepared for a short term involvement? Please explain.
_____

Thank you

Implementation

STAGE I

In a copy of the Temple Bulletin, the President should announce the formation
of a Human Resources Committee, and ask for people to contact the Temple office
if they would be interested in serving.

STAGE II

In the next Temple Bulletin (next month), a letter should appear from the
Chairperson of the Human Resources Committee, explaining that there will be a
Human Resources Questionnaire sent to members of the Congregation, and stating
what it is designed to accomplish, and thanking people for their support.

STAGE III

The questionnaire can then be circulated to the members of the Congregation.
In each of the Bulletins, subsequent to Stage II, for a period of 2 or 3 months,
there should be a reminder to the members of the Congregation to send in their
questionnaire, and on the last reminder, a sincere thank you for their assistance.

STAGE IV

The data on the profile should be transferred to a file card system or a
computer data bank in a manner that will facilitate information recovery. All
people who have indicated a desire to become involved should be called immediately
to thank them and confirm that they can get involved. They should be told that
they will be contacted as soon as possible.

STAGE V

The Human Resources Committee must compile and distribute to the appropriate
locations the names of congregants who have expressed interest in Temple life
stating what their interest is and what information we have on their Human
Resources Profile. Any programme suggestions should be listed and circulated to
both laity and staff so that they can be placed on the appropriate Agendas.

AFFIRMATION:
Adult Confirmation and Re-Confirmation Program

The ACADEMY is delighted to announce a new opportunity for adult members of Temple Israel to continue their Jewish education by participating in the Adult Affirmation program.

What are the requirements? A commitment to continuing adult Jewish Education and 36 credits of approved study.

What constitutes approved study? A student can choose from the following options.

OPTION A

Earn all 36 credits by taking 12 ACADEMY courses, each one of which is 3 credits.

OPTION B

Become an Adult Bar or Bat Mitzvah and begin the Affirmation program with 12 credits. Earn the remaining 24 credits by taking 8 ACADEMY courses or a *minimum* of 7 ACADEMY courses and participating in a combination of the following:

✔ a Temple Israel Adult Retreat, 1 credit;

✔ a Hebrew Union College - Jewish Institute of Religion Zimmerman Institute, 1 credit;

✔ a Union of American Hebrew Congregations Summer Kallah, 1 credit; or

✔ regular attendance at Temple Israel's Rebbe's tisch, 1 credit.

OPTION C

Earn 33 credits by taking 11 ACADEMY courses and the remaining 3 credits by participating in a combination of the opportunities listed in Option B.

When will the first class be confirmed? Spring, 1993.

To register as a Program participant, sign up on the ACADEMY registration form on page 6.

BIBLIOGRAPHY

A Facilitator Training Manual for Connecting Purpose, Process and People (UAHC Commission on Synagogue Management Task Force on Leadership Development: NY, NY), Revised February 1987

Fein, Leonard J., et. al. *Reform Is A Verb,* (Long Range Planning Committee of the UAHC: NY, NY), 1972

Oswald, Roy. M. and Speed B. Leas, *The Inviting Church* (The Alban Institute, Inc.: Washington, DC), 1987.

Rothauge, Arlin J., *Sizing Up A Congregation For New Member Ministry,* (The Episcopal Church Center: NY, NY)

The Clergy Journal, March 1990 (Church Management, Inc.: Austin, TX)

Wengrow, Irv, "Membership Recruitment, Involvement and Retention", Rev. February 1991, UAHC Department of Small Congregations and UAHC Ida & Howard Wilkoff Department of Synagogue Management